Praise for
Hearth and Home Witchcraft

"Jennie's blend of witchcraft and hygge resonates so deeply with me. In *Hearth and Home Witchcraft*, Jennie shares her personal practice as a means to inspire readers to approach their daily life as magical and spiritual. Nourishment and comfort are important themes here, as is accessibility; you don't need a background in magick to start exploring hearth-craft. Jennie's book is a joyful and supportive exploration of domestic witchcraft."

—Arin Murphy-Hiscock, author of *The House Witch*,
The Green Witch, and other books

"*Hearth and Home Witchcraft* is everything I wanted—practical, grounded, and utterly magical. For anyone who can't quite figure out how to be a witch and live in the world, Jennie Blonde offers a guide to incorporating magic into the everyday, making the simplest of moments meaningful and powerful."

—Nikki Van De Car, author of *Practical Magic*
and *The Witchy Homestead*

"This lovely book is packed with recipes, rituals, and spells for every season and occasion. Jennie walks you through a day and a year in the life of a real, modern witch, integrating the magickal and the mundane with a flick of her wand, (or wooden spoon). If you've been wondering how to turn your daily life into a cozy embodiment of magick, then this book is for you!"

—Tenae Stewart, author of *The Modern Witch's Guide to Natural Magick*

"*Hearth and Home Witchcraft* is a comfy, cozy book packed with splendid rituals and fabulous recipes. On every page, you'll find fun ideas to awaken your magical inspiration."

—Tess Whitehurst, author of *Magical Housekeeping*

Hearth & Home Witchcraft

Hearth & Home Witchcraft

Rituals and Recipes to Nourish Home and Spirit

JENNIE BLONDE

The "Comfy Cozy Witch"

WEISER
BOOKS

This edition first published in 2022 by Weiser Books, an imprint of
Red Wheel/Weiser, LLC
With offices at:
65 Parker Street, Suite 7
Newburyport, MA 01950
www.redwheelweiser.com

ISBN: 978-1-57863-773-7
Library of Congress Cataloging-in-Publication Data available upon request.

Cover painting, "Aga with Pestle and Mortar, 1997, John Napper © 2022 Artists
Rights Society (ARS), New York / DACS, London.
Private Collection/Bridgeman Images

Typeset in Adobe Text Pro

Printed in United States of America
IBI
10 9 8 7 6 5 4 3 2 1

To all the comfy cozy witches out there.
And to the practitioners who came before me;
thank you for forging the path.

Book Charm

I want to be sure you get the most out of this book, so if you would like, here's a charm to enchant this book and your reading of it.

Place the book in your left hand with your right hand on top. Speak the following words aloud while imagining a warm golden light encapsulating the book.

May my reading experience be comforting and warm.
May this book help me see magic in the everyday to bring protection,
joy, and nourishment to my home, family, and friends.
Be it so.

Contents

Chapter 1:
Hearth and Home Witchcraft

CHAPTER 2:
IN THE HOME

CHAPTER 3:
IN THE KITCHEN

CHAPTER 4:
IN THE SACRED SPACE

CHAPTER 5:

THE GARDEN AND NATURE

CHAPTER 6:
SELF-CARE

CHAPTER 7:
EVERYDAY RITUALS

LIST OF RITUALS AND RECIPES

Acknowledgments

First, a huge thank you to the comfy cozy witch community. Your support has been overwhelming, and I am honored to call many of you friends. I never would have considered writing this book without the support of so many of you!

Thank you to my former agent, Sarah Landis, for being a constant cheerleader of my work, no matter how many genres I choose to write in! And a major thanks to the entire team at Weiser, especially Peter, for your continued support and cheerleading for this book. I couldn't imagine my debut nonfiction experience being any better—truly!

Thank you to all my friends and family for your support—especially to my aunt, Tante, who loves talking about all things witchy with me . . . at least twice a day.

To my husband, Eddie, for holding down the fort late nights, weekends, and when I escape for much-needed writing retreats—thank you. And to my son, B, who reminds me to find the magic in every single thing every single day. May you never lose that sense of wonder and magic. I love you both so, so much.

And finally, to my late grandparents—Nana, Peeps, Grammy, and Pappy. Your support from beyond is felt and appreciated. Thank you for being with me as I write all the words. Love you.

INTRODUCTION

When I opened my personal Instagram account, the first thing I was asked to provide was a username, which often is the most difficult part of starting any account. I wanted something that represented me, my craft, and where I was currently in my practice. I thought about my favorite parts of my personal practice—my daily ritual in the early mornings at my altar with a cup of coffee and candles; journaling in my book of shadows and pulling cards from my favorite decks of tarot and oracle cards; time spent in the kitchen speaking blessings and intention into the food that nourishes my family; spring and summer days spent in the garden tending to herbs and plants, asking them to grow; hours of hiking in the local woods, watching the birds and small animals come and go; and evenings in front of the fireplace, curled up under a blanket with my dogs at my side, a mug of tea in my hands, reading the latest witchy book release. Reflecting on those things that have become such integral parts of my practice made me realize they all have something in common—a thread of comfort and calm—which led to the perfect words, the perfect name, to encapsulate who I am—a Comfy Cozy Witch.

I firmly believe that every witch's craft is constantly evolving, changing as they grow in their spirituality and their practice. That certainly was the case for me. When I began practicing, there weren't subgenres of witchcraft. I remember a witch being either a solitary practitioner or in a coven, pagan or not. When I started out, I was simply a solitary witch, lover of all things witchy and magical, who found myself in the very back of the broom closet. But over the years and through the ebbs and flows of my craft, through times of practicing daily and practicing very little, one thing that was always true for me was the fact that my witchcraft was always grounding and comforting for me. And when I would step away from it, any time I came back, magic enveloped me in warmth and comfort. It was a place I could come home to. Although I've been practicing my witchy ways on and off for over two decades, it wasn't until the past few years that I found my niche—combining witchcraft with *hygge*, creating something (as I often say in my posts or on my podcast) comfy, cozy, and witchy.

Witchcraft in and of itself is comforting. Sure, there are not-so-comfortable parts as well—working with the shadow, coming face to face with that which holds you back, having to let go of things you once loved yet realized don't serve you. But beyond some of the more difficult parts of the practice, to me witchcraft is about honoring my home, family, and self-care practices; connecting with nature, with my higher self, with something beyond, whether that be deity, universe, spirit, etc.; and being comfortable in all aspects of myself.

In times of anxiety, I turn to my practice. When I need a moment of calm and reflection, I retreat to my sacred space for quiet meditation, card pulls, and journaling to nourish my soul. When I want to nourish my family, I turn to my garden and herbs and cooking grimoire and cauldron (my stockpot) for a bit of kitchen witchery. When I wish to nourish my body, I turn to mindful movement and self-care rituals and spell work. And throughout the day, every day, there are small rituals I perform to keep me connected to my practice. It's all of those things together that is the heart of my craft.

As I said before, the craft is ever-evolving. Something I've noticed over the past few years is how much the aesthetic of witchcraft has been emphasized—elaborate altars filled with tools, technical videos of spellcasting with smoke billowing in the background, coven photo shoots with make-up and expensive outfits—an aesthetic born of lore and pop culture and the sometimes intangible standards of social media. Although I love seeing that very aesthetic part of the craft, and at times do recreate some of it myself, that piece is not the heart of the practice for me and is, in fact, unattainable to many witches. What comfy cozy witchery is about is making the craft accessible. Adding comforting ritual into the everyday to stay connected to your practice in small, attainable ways.

When thinking about the structure of this book, I decided to go to my own practice—to sit in nature, meditate, journal, and do a bit of divination. I went to the spot in nature that makes me feel the most grounded and connected to my craft—the woods. In the dead of winter, I threw on my hat, heavy jacket, and gloves, grabbed a journal from my sacred space, and headed out. What did I wish to convey through this book? What tone did I want it to have?

The answer was simple—when people read this book, I want them to feel as if they're chatting with a witchy friend at the kitchen table over a cup of hot tea. A blend of story-telling, witchcraft, and warmth in a book accessible to any witch, at any point in their journey. A book filled with information, personal anecdotes, rituals, spell work, and recipes to nourish yourself, nourish your home, and nourish your spirit.

It's my hope you'll take some of the ideas, rituals, and recipes from this book and apply them to your own practice to help you feel more connected, grounded, and nourished in your home, in your body, and in your spirit.

Blessed Be.

CHAPTER 1

Hearth and Home Witchcraft

They say home is where the heart is.
I say, home is where the magic is.

—JENNIE BLONDE

What's in a Name?

Before we get started, there's something I want to say. This book is for any-one—whether you call yourself a witch or not—who wants to create a comfy, cozy, and magical life. It's for the witch who is new to the craft and learning and for the witch who's been practicing for years and wants a nudge, a little help, to refresh their practice. It's also for the person who wants to find small, meaningful ways to stay connected to their innate magic, to discover a new side of spirituality, to create a magical home filled with ritual and meaning.

At its core, comfy cozy witchcraft is all about finding and practicing com-forting and nourishing hearth and home magic.

Hearth and home witchery has been a phrase tossed around a lot in the past few years, as the witchy world has felt the need to create labels for their particular approach to the craft, but what exactly is it? To me, hearth and home witchery is about seeing the home as a sacred space, a place of safety, nourishment, and magic. It's about finding the magic in the every-day goings-on of home and of life, no matter how mundane they may seem: cooking, cleaning, reading, relaxing, gardening, spending time with family, and even sleeping. It's about not putting too much on yourself to create an *aesthetic* of crafting, but being in touch with your innate power and practice in small, meaningful ways.

I read somewhere recently, and I wish I could remember the source, that hearth craft can be a blend of green witchcraft and house witchcraft, bringing together the natural world and the mundane to create magic in a comforting, calming way. It's magic that is very much rooted in the home, in the kitchen, and in the earth. And it's magic that focuses on *you* and the environment you create, rather than relying on outside forces to create change.

What Is a Comfy Cozy House Witch?

A number of people have reached out to me to ask, "What do I need to be a comfy cozy witch?" When I'm asked this, I laugh (not in their faces, of course, but to myself). First, although I am the "Comfy Cozy Witch," I find it funny that people think there is a specific way to be one. There are no ingredients or tools that make me one other than the fact that this is how I identify myself, and every person can choose to identify themselves in whichever way they want.

Sometimes what makes me a comfy cozy witch is sipping on a cup of peppermint tea and reciting a few pieces of verse aloud. Other times, it's doing a full-moon ritual in my outdoor sacred space. And other times, it's as simple as popping in my ear buds and listening to a guided meditation to put me to sleep. That's what I love so much about being a witch—there is no single way to be one.

> *"House and home witchcraft is comfy cozy grounding at its core."*

However, if I'm pressed and asked to pinpoint some items for home, hearth, and comfy cozy witchery, there are a few that come in mind.

Grounding. House and home witchcraft is comfy and cozy grounding at its core, related to the root chakra, the deep burgundies and reds and autumnal hues, and the mug of magical tea in your hands. To me, being safe and secure and *grounded* is the basis to any magical working. Whether you're stirring intention into that early morning cup of coffee, taking a moment to connect with the tarot for guidance during the workday, curling up under a blanket with the latest book on spirituality, taking a stroll through your garden with your furry friend, or lighting a candle at the end of a long day, all these actions create a sense of warmth, security, comfort, and are innately grounding. I mean, just think about how satisfying that first sip of coffee is each morning and how quickly it brings you into the present moment. The witchcraft and practices surrounding house and hearth is inherently grounding and comforting.

Although I don't like to define my kind of practice (as it's ever-changing), my witchcraft is rooted in hearth, home, and nature—and there are a few basics items I tend to in my personal practice that will be addressed throughout this book—celebrating the sabbats, spending time in a natural setting, creating and visiting sacred spaces, protecting and cleansing my home, nurturing my family with healthy nourishing food, and establishing daily rituals and self-care routines that keep me connected to my practice, mindful of the present moment, and in tune with my magical self.

Safety. To me, a large part of hearth and home witchcraft is creating an environment of safety and comfort. I say this fully understanding the privilege I have in being able to do this, as I live in a relatively safe area to begin with. There are many who live in an environment or place they wouldn't consider safe. But it's important to note that safety is more than just the place or the physical space. When I speak of safety and protection, I'm talking about creating an energetic space of protection. I do this using clearing, cleansing, and protection rituals that I'll be sharing with you in the next chapter and beyond. I firmly believe that magic can't be performed when we're in a space of anxiety and stress, and by protecting ourselves, our sacred spaces, and our tools, the true magic in our craft will shine through.

PROTECTION HERBS, SPICES, AND STONES

For centuries, people have been using a variety of stones, herbs, and spices in their witch-craft, food, and protection rituals to help keep unwanted spirits and entities at bay. Below are some stones to place around your property, in the corners of your homes, or in your car for protection. Use the herbs and spices in your recipes, teas, and other items to enhance protection. Draw the symbols on items you wish to protect as well.

- *Herbs: dill, lavender, parsley, oregano, rosemary, comfrey, sage, basil, mugwort, vervain*
- *Spices: cinnamon, red pepper, black pepper, salt*
- *Stones: black obsidian, shungite, tiger's eye, pyrite, labradorite, smoky quartz, black tourmaline*
- *Symbols: pentacle, handmade sigils*

Nourishment. Chapter 3 will discuss in detail kitchen witchery, complete with rituals and recipes. But an important ingredient to my practice is nour-ishment: nourishing my body with healthy foods from the earth and with regular exercise and mindful movement; nourishing my mind through read-ing, meditation, and decompression; and nourishing my spirit through daily ritual work. As a house witch, I take nourishment to the next level and find ways to nourish my family—my husband, son, and two fur babies. All of these are important parts of my practice as a comfy cozy house witch.

Self-care. Oh . . . self-care is one of the most important aspects of my prac-tice because if I'm not taking care of myself, how can I possibly practice to the best of my ability? And if I'm not caring for myself, then how can I care for others, whether that be my people or my animals, in my home? Chapter 7 will detail self-care rituals, spells, and recipes to up your magical self-care game, but if you put this book down before getting to that chapter, take this as a sign to check in with yourself and ask if your mundane and spiritual self-care needs have been met.

Sacred Space. Sacred space is so much more than altar space. It's where we come to connect with deity, spirit, higher self, source, etc. It's a place of calm and comfort that immediately takes us out of our heads and into the present. A place where we can get grounded for work. A place to connect with ancestors. Sacred space can be your home, a room, a balcony, your garden, a windowsill, or even yourself. When I need to connect to my practice in a comfortable way, I make my way to one of my many sacred spaces.

Attitude. You'll see me come back to this many times throughout this book. Much of what we do depends on our attitudes. I've heard many people say (admittedly, myself included), "Oh, it's going to be one of *those* days!" When we say things like this, we're setting ourselves up for "that kind of day." When we choose to focus on what goes wrong, we're putting that thought out there in the world, basically asking the universe to match our thoughts.

But, if we approach the day and obstacles with a bit of optimism and positivity, then maybe we'll have a better result. Don't get me wrong . . . I know there is a threshold where positivity can become toxic. But I'm not talking about being positive all the time. I'm speaking of the need to check in with yourself once in a while and check in with your attitude. We can't always control what happens to us, but we can control *how we react* to what happens to us.

Grace. There is nothing comfy or cozy about guilt and feeling shame for doing or not doing something. That's why it's important to not beat yourself up for skipping a few days of meditation, card pulls, kitchen witchery, or whatever your practice looks like to you. I think it's also important to remember that sometimes the mundane outweighs the magical—the jobs, the cleaning, raising children, and the like—but house and home witchcraft is about being okay with those mundane parts of your life and finding a way to bring bits of magic into them.

All of these items we'll be exploring throughout this book, but first, I want to introduce you to the hearth and home deities, faeries, angels, and spirits we can look to for guidance, protection, and all-around comfort in our homes.

HEARTH AND HOME DEITIES, FAERIES, AND SPIRITS

Although by no means necessary, many domestic witches choose to work with a household deity (either on its own or in addition to other deity work). You may choose to work with a particular domestic god or goddess or perhaps an animistic deity—an entity or spirit of your local lands. Deities of hearth and home look out for the home, property, and members of the household, including pets and outdoor animals. Even if you work with a particular deity in your everyday magical workings, consider petitioning a household deity for the protection and safety of your family, animals, and indoor and outdoor property.

Choosing a Deity

Before you choose to work with any domestic deity, or a deity in general, it's important to do your due diligence in the form of research. Read up on particular deities or ask your witch friends about their experiences with household deities (assuming that's something they're comfortable sharing with you). There's no single way to approach every deity, so that is where research is key. And if you wish to work with a member of the fae (particularly brownies, as they're household faeries known to be a bit mischievous), make sure you proceed with caution, and, again, do your research.

I have to admit, although I've worked with Brigid and Hestia (arguably the most well-known domestic goddesses) and members of the "fair folk," until doing research for this book, I wasn't aware of some of the other deities associated, some closely, with house and home and kitchen witchcraft. Below, I'll chat about some of the most common domestic deities. Although not a complete list, consider the following a good starting place.

HESTIA

Hestia, known as the "first of all divinities to be invoked" (meaning the first deity of the twelve original Olympians), is the Greek goddess of hearth and home and domesticity. Although there aren't many myths associated with Hestia, it's said that her parents, Cronus and Rhea, confined her to the home, her sole job being to tend to the flame. Her name means "hearth" and speaks to the sacred element of fire that was so important to the Greek deities.

Although there are few representations through artwork of Hestia, she is typically portrayed as a woman in the mother phase of her life, wearing a veil while standing by a large fire and holding flowers in her hand. The myths and folklore surrounding gods and goddesses were told to explain occurrences in the natural world. It's thought, and has even been said by Aristotle, that the crackling of the fire is the sound of Hestia laughing.

I call on Hestia (and the deity I'll be talking about next) when I'm in need of connecting to my house—cooking, cleaning, domesticity. Hestia is also a great deity to work with when you're in need of security, warmth, wellbeing, family connection, abundance, and harmony in the house and home.

Hestia's correspondences include the element of fire, the cow and pig, the peacock, and she relates to the signs of Aries and Virgo.

VESTA

Vesta, a Roman domestic goddess, is considered the equivalent of the Greek goddess Hestia. She's the goddess of hearth and fires and, very much like Hestia, was worshipped in every Roman household as the first deity. Offerings of food thrown directly into the fire were made to honor her. Her correspondences are the same as Hestia's, and you can reach out to her by working with those correspondences.

BRIGID

Brigid is one of my favorite goddesses to work with, as she is not only the Celtic goddess of home and the forge but also a goddess of inspiration. And as an author of nonfiction and fiction, I am always in need of a bit of inspiration. Brigid is the goddess of healing, fertility, and poetry. Known as "The Bright One," Brigid is associated with sacred wells, rivers, fires, fertility, music, communication, warmth, and well-being (to name only a few). The pagan celebration Imbolc, the midway point between the winter solstice and the spring equinox, is dedicated to Brigid.

I call on Brigid when I'm in need of healing for myself or for my family. I find the best way to connect with her is by pouring myself a cup of something warm, pouring a second cup as an offering to her, and then gently talking with her about what it is I seek. Brigid and I have had many cups of tea together over the years.

Brigid's symbol is the cauldron, her element fire and direction south; her day is Sunday, and you can wear peridot, azurite, or Brigid's cross to feel connected to her energy. She's associated with oak, rowan, willow, and blackthorn trees, and her animals include bear, sheep, chicken, and swan.

GABIJA

Gabija is the spirit embodiment of the fire in Lithuanian mythology; her name derives from *gaubti,* which means "to protect." Like Hestia, she is the protector of home and all its inhabitants and is known to take on the forms of a rooster or cat. The fire dedicated to Gabija was never allowed to be put out, except during the summer solstice festivities when a new fire was created. Coals from the fire were passed around Lithuania by a human chain of women, transporting the fire through villages and into homes.

Gabija is known especially for her protection over animals; she is associated with the colors burgundy and red and enjoys offerings of salty breads and other starches.

FORNAX

Fornax is a house and hearth goddess who was considered in ancient Rome to be the personification of the oven and cooking hearth. She's known to keep bread and other baked goods from burning and to prevent fire from destroying homes. She's the deity to call upon when you're doing any baking in the oven (or if you're in need of a bit of baking help). In ancient Rome, families would hold feasts complete with fruit, fresh breads, and cakes (a festival called Fornacalia) as a thank you to Fornax for her blessing over the hearth.

BROWNIES

These Celtic faeries are often seen as being short in stature, hardworking, and helpful. Brownies are house faeries thought to come into homes during the night to clean and tidy while residents sleep. Brownies are especially helpful with domestic tasks and providing support when one is doing any type of arduous housework.

When working with brownies, don't expect too much of them or ask them to do all your housework. If you ask too much of them without offering them something in return, they are known to make a ruckus and a mess during the night—banging pots and pans together or dumping cups of milk or boxes of cereal and oatmeal. Brownies adore family pets and animals, and the energy of little children makes them happy. In fact, it's those children and animals who may be the first in the household to recognize the presence of brownies.

Brownies' powers include loyalty, magic, order and organization, responsibility, and accomplishment. They are associated with the color brown, their insect is the bee (honey is an important offering to the fae), and their element is earth.

HOBGOBLINS

Also known as hobs, these are the English version of brownies who spend much of their time in the family's kitchen or at the hearth. Once thought to be the spirit of the hearth, or guardian of the fireside, these faeries are known to bond with particular families and stay loyal to those families, moving from home to home as the family does.

Hobgoblins are most satisfied tending to their chosen families and take joy in helping them with daily goings-on. But just like other brownies, make a hob upset and you can say goodbye to important objects, especially shiny ones—car and house keys, jewelry, and loose change.

LARES AND PENATES

Although lesser known, Lares and Penates, or Di Penates, were Roman household spirits (or gods) known to safeguard the home and anything related to the health, nourishment, and protection of family and the items within a home. Penates, in particular, oversee the storage of food and pantry, helping to keep foods from going stale. The ancient Romans were known to have figures or dollies near the hearth as representations of the Penates. They're associated with crossroads, family, protection, prosperity, and well-being.

ARCHANGEL GABRIEL

Commonly known as being the "strength of God," Gabriel is connected to the house and home in his work with healing, hope, renewal, discipline, and order/organization. To honor Gabriel and ask him for guidance when considering a move, major purchase, or renovations, plant lilies or olive trees; use the colors aqua, sea green, and white on your altar/décor; and wear onyx or quartz gemstones. Gabriel is associated with Monday, the element earth, dusk, cats, and owls.

Rituals and Blessings

House Goddess Ritual

To invoke the assistance of the hearth goddesses and invite these domestic deities into your home, try this house goddess ritual. You may perform this ritual in any area of your home you feel is best suitable to call on a domestic deity; for example, kitchen, living room, or hearth. The area you choose must have a flat surface to set your candle. Perform this ritual as many times as you'd like throughout the year or whenever you feel your home is in need of some extra protection and love from Goddess.

You'll need:

    one brown candle

    1 tablespoon rosemary

    a pinch of salt

    matches or a lighter

Place the candle on a flat dish in your chosen space. Sprinkle the rosemary and salt in a circle around the candle. Light the candle and watch the flame flicker and dance while saying:

Deities of domesticity, I light this candle for you,

A representation of hearth and home.

Bless this house and all within

With protection and warmth.

Wait for the candle to burn down, then close the ritual by saying:

By the powers of fire and earth,

This spell is spoke and sealed.

Be it so.

House Faery Blessing

Light a white candle and speak the following blessing before settling down for the night.

Faeries of home and hearth, I send you gratitude.

Continue to watch over my family and beloved pet(s).

By the home and hearth this blessing is spoke.

For the highest good, and with harm to none.

A Warming Incense to Invoke Hestia

As Hestia is my hearth goddess of choice, it's only natural that I include an incense used to invoke her, the sacred goddess of the fire and the forge. Use this incense in the evening before settling down in front of the fire or before any workings where you need her assistance.

You'll need:

¼ cup red sandalwood powder

¼ cup cedar chips

6 drops amber essential oil

3 drops jasmine essential oil

2 drops cinnamon essential oil

1 teaspoon chamomile flowers

Mix the sandalwood and cedar chips in a bowl. Add the essential oils and chamomile flowers. Blend together. Burn the incense mixture on a charcoal tablet and say, "I invoke you, Hestia, to be a reminder of the warmth and joy in this home and hearth space and of the innate warmth within. Thank you." Enjoy the heady scent of warmth and magic.

THE WHEEL OF THE YEAR

As a domestic witch with a knack for kitchen witchery, I have to admit I am at my prime comfy cozy witchiness during the sabbat celebrations! The term "sabbat" originated in Wicca but is now used by Wiccan and non-Wiccan practitioners alike. These eight festivals celebrate the turning of the wheel, the birth-life-death circle, and the planting, growing, harvest, and death of crops. The festivals also encompass the four main solar events of the solstices and equinoxes and the four midpoints between them.

"There's no better time to nourish and enjoy those in your life than on the Sabbats"

It's during these celebrations when families gather, covens meet, seasonal food is cooked, and rituals are performed. Domestic witchiness at its best. There's no better time to nourish and enjoy those in your life than on the sabbats. (Oh, and if you're in the broom closet, nobody will question you making a seasonal meal!)

Before each sabbat celebration, I perform an energetic and physical cleanse of my house. I do this to ensure a clean and vibrant home for celebrating (and, if you're like me, I am not ready to practice until my space is organized and clean, or else all I can think about is my mess!). I also prepare a menu for each festival that celebrates the current growth season. I decorate my everyday altar with correspondences associated with the particular sabbat, and I prepare for some sort of ritual, big or small, depending on time and season.

There is no need to put on a big show, as a sabbat celebration doesn't need to be a huge to-do. For example, my summer celebrations are often smaller

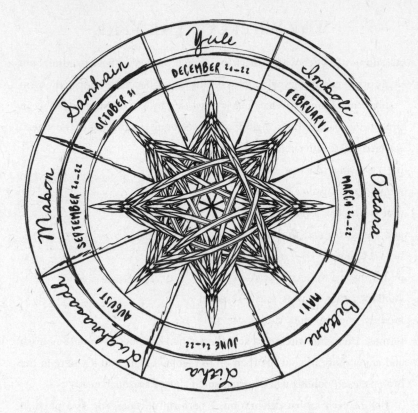

because of vacations, limited time to cook, etc. Below you'll find a brief overview of each sabbat, some ideas for celebrating, and their correspondences for reference. This is a good place to start if you're new to the Wheel of the Year or is a nice little refresher for you more experienced witches.

Samhain (October 31–November 1)

Let's start with the sabbat considered *the "Witches' New Year."* Samhain is arguably the favorite sabbat of most witches, and it's the one most associated with witchcraft. Samhain is celebrated around Halloween, and during this festival, passed loved ones—friends, family, and pets—are honored and celebrated.

The veil between worlds is thinnest at this celebration, making it the perfect time for ancestor work and for connecting to those who've passed on. It's the ideal sabbat for tending to loved ones' grave sites and for divination work. Samhain is associated with endings in our lives, so it's a time to contemplate what things are no longer serving you and what relationships should come to a close. Samhain season is one of introspection and reflection on what in your life needs to be released so you can move forward into the new year.

Samhain is also the third and final harvest celebration on the Wheel of the Year when root vegetables, beans, and pumpkins are gathered and stored for the colder months. This is a great time to complete spell work for banishing and release, protection, past lives, and ancestral healing. Oh, and divination work is in its prime during Samhain, so get out those cards, runes, pendulums, scrying implements, and the like.

Many witches use this time to create an ancestor altar, do cemetery walks, carve and decorate pumpkins and other squash, and share family stories. Many pagans who celebrate the god/goddess honor the goddess as "crone" at Samhain. The god isn't present, as he's waiting to be reborn at Yule.

SAMHAIN CORRESPONDENCES

Colors: black, orange

Trees: pomegranate, willow, hazel, yew, blackthorn

Herbs: allspice, catnip, cinnamon, mugwort, garlic, sage

Gemstones: carnelian, obsidian, onyx, bloodstone

Animals: bat, cat, dog, boar

Intentions: ancestors, crone wisdom, crossroads, death, divination, introspection, vision

Ways to celebrate: go for a cemetery walk, decorate with seasonal imagery, put together an ancestor altar, host a Feast of the Dead, share stories and reflections of passed loved ones, use divination tools for guidance, perform some bonfire magic

Samhain Recipe: Candied Squash

Ingredients:

3 cups peeled and diced butternut squash

3 tablespoons unsalted butter

2 teaspoons brown sugar

½ teaspoon cinnamon

½ teaspoon nutmeg

½ teaspoon salt

¼ teaspoon black pepper

Directions:

1. Cook the squash in a pot of boiling water with a dash of salt until squash is tender (7–9 minutes). Remove from heat and drain.

2. Melt the butter in a large skillet over medium heat. Add the sugar and spice mixture. Stir until mixture begins to thicken (about 2 minutes).

3. Add the squash, coating it well with the butter/sugar/spice mixture. Stir for two minutes. Remove from heat.

4. Plate and garnish with fresh rosemary.

Ancestor Honoring Ritual

This simple ritual is one I perform each Samhain at dinnertime. My nana passed in 2021, so last Samhain was an extra special time for my family to reminisce, telling stories of our outings to the hidden park down the street, cups of sweet tea on Nana's watermelon-decorated screened-in porch, or the time she took my best friend and me to New York City and stayed out until two in the morning (my nana was a fun one!).

Perform this ritual on the evening of October 31 or November 1.

1. Prepare you Samhain dinner as usual.

2. Set the table and place an extra setting out for your ancestors.

3. Place three black candles in the middle of the dinner table and light them.

4. Ask your family members to join hands. If you're performing the ritual alone, hold your hands out to the side, palms up.

5. Say: *Tonight we honor our ancestors and call out to those who came before. Ancestors of the highest good, we welcome you and thank you for your protection and guidance. Please share this meal with us.*

6. Serve dinner, making sure to first serve the ancestor's place setting and then everyone else. Over dinner, reminisce and share stories of passed loved ones with others at the table.

7. Once you've finished the meal, say: *We thank you, ancestors, for celebrating with us tonight. Although dead, you continue to live on with us. Blessed Be.*

Yule/Winter Solstice (December 21–23)

Yule (originally called Jul), marked by the winter solstice, is a festival that takes place on the longest night of the year. The focus of this sabbat is not only darkness but also the return of the light and eventual end of winter, as from here on the days will ever so slowly grow longer.

Although Yule is about festivities and the celebration of the return of the light, it also marks the beginning of the coldest months ahead. Centuries ago, Norse peoples knew that many cold and barren days were ahead of them at this time of year, so they asked deities to provide them with protection and strength for the coming months.

The festivities of Yule focus on the fire and the hearth (the domestic witch in me loves this!). Many cultures around the world have their own celebrations of the winter solstice and the return of light—the Christian Christmas traditions (adapted from the pagan Yule festival and Roman Saturnalia), Hannukah with its lighting of the menorah, and Kwanzaa and the candle-lighting festivities. Candles are symbolic of this light, and the round evergreen wreaths symbolize the circle of life. At this time, the goddess ("mother" in the maiden-mother-crone cycle) gives birth to the infant god as part of the birth/growth/death/rebirth cycle. With his birth, hope is born once again, bringing warmth out of the cold.

Yule is a time of festivities, merriment, celebrating, gathering, and gratitude. A time for loved ones to celebrate the season, celebrate the return of the sun, celebrate camaraderie of family and friends, and a time of giving.

YULE CORRESPONDENCES

Colors: green, red, white, silver, gold

Animals: bear, eagle, owl, deer, snow goose

Trees: fir, holly, pine, cedar, spruce, birch, yew, oak

Scents: cedar, peppermint, clove, cinnamon, frankincense

Gemstones: bloodstone, emerald, ruby, garnet, moss agate, snowflake obsidian

Herbs: rosemary, thyme, cinnamon, peppermint, clove, nutmeg, bayberry

Food: mulled wine, wassail, squash, root vegetables, meat, breads

Ways to celebrate: build a Yule altar, create and burn a Yule log, decorate a Yule tree, celebrate the festival by candlelight, make an evergreen wreath, exchange gifts made from nature, host a holiday party

Yule Recipe: Spiced Wassail

Ingredients:

3 cups cranberry juice

4 cups apple cider

2 cinnamon sticks

1 orange studded with cloves

1 sliced apple

1 teaspoon cinnamon

½ teaspoon nutmeg

¼ cup brown sugar

Directions:

1. Mix all ingredients together on the stovetop or in a slow cooker.

2. Bring to a simmer and let steep for 3–5 minutes.

3. Serve hot and enjoy!

Imbolc (February 1–2)

Imbolc, a cross-quarter celebration, is the first of the three fertility sabbats, with Ostara and Beltane being the other two; it is also the first of the four Celtic fire festivals, which include Beltane, Lughnasadh, and Samhain. Imbolc represents the seed that begins the wheels turning in the Wheel of the Year and is a celebration of the ever-lengthening days and the transition from winter to spring. At this time, the seeds of life are just beginning to spring underground, even if we can't see them yet.

Because Imbolc is associated with the stirrings of spring, it's a time to think about growth and change and what you might want to bring to fruition in the coming weeks and months. Because the name Imbolc means "in the belly" (referring to the gestation period of the ewe), it's a time when hope and change is stirred within. Magical workings surrounding Imbolc include newness, creation, increasing love in your household, creating prosperity and abundance, and welcoming personal growth.

Imbolc is here to remind you of your inner spark of power and determination through the final weeks of winter. At Imbolc, the goddess returns in her maiden form—young, new, full of hope and wonder, and the god is slowly growing from an infant into a child.

Many pagans celebrate the Celtic goddess Brigid at this time (myself included), as she's the overseer of transformation, fertility, crafts, poetry, inspiration, and house and home.

IMBOLC CORRESPONDENCES

Colors: white, silver, green, yellow

Animals: lamb, sheep, cow, goat, winter birds, dog, groundhog

Trees: rowan, birch, willow

Scents: honey, rosemary, cinnamon, frankincense

Gemstones: snow quartz, moss agate, goldstone, charoite, fire agate, ruby

Herbs: rosemary, basil, bay, angelica, chamomile, lavender

Food: braided breads, milk, cheese, cakes, wine, lamb

Ways to celebrate: make a Brigid straw doll to honor the Celtic goddess of fire and fertility, host a feast, have a bonfire, visit a body of water, cleanse your home, decorate your altar

☘ ⚬ ☘

Imbolc Recipe: Honey Butter

This butter is a deliciously sweet addition to your dinner rolls, herby breads, and other baked goods. Bonus—it takes no time to whip up!

Ingredients:

> 8 ounces softened unsalted butter
>
> ¼ cup honey
>
> 1 tablespoon powdered sugar
>
> ¼ teaspoon sea salt

Directions:

1. Place softened butter in a bowl or mixer. Using a hand mixer or stand mixer, beat the butter until smooth.

2. Add remaining ingredients and continue beating at medium speed. Be sure to scrape down the sides of the bowl as needed. Finish once all ingredients are fully incorporated and butter is smooth.

3. Add additional honey or salt depending on your desired taste.

4. Serve while it's still warm or refrigerate it for a later use. Store up to a week.

Add a dash of warmth and protection magic to the butter by adding cinnamon.

Ostara/Spring Equinox (March 20–22)

Ostara is the second of the fertility sabbats and is also known as spring equinox—a time of equal light and dark, day and night. This spring sabbat gets its name from Eostre, the Saxon goddess of spring and fertility and sounds very much like the Christian Easter. In fact, Ostara is the origin of many traditions now associated with Easter—those adorable rabbits and baby peeps that symbolize new life and growth.

Like the fall equinox (which we'll get to in a few pages), this is a time of balance—the balance of darkness and light, of female and male energies as the maiden grows and the god is reaching his manhood, of inner and outer self, and of the physical and spiritual world. A fire festival celebrating the ever-returning sun, Ostara celebrates growth, rebirth, renewal, and beginnings. It's the perfect time to reevaluate, once again, what is no longer serving you, release that, and focus on what you want to grow in your personal, home, and spiritual life.

OSTARA CORRESPONDENCES

Colors: pastels of green, yellow, pink, red, robin's egg blue

Animals: bunny, chick, robin, lamb, snake

Flowers: lily, jasmine, peony, narcissus, violet, daisy, forsythia

Herbs: chamomile, lavender, ginger

Gemstones: amethyst, citrine, moonstone, aquamarine, rose quartz, clear quartz

Scents: honeysuckle, lavender, hyacinth

Food: breads, eggs, cheese, honey, wine

Ways to celebrate: go bird watching; dye Ostara eggs; plant seeds for your vegetable, flower, or herb garden; take a nature walk and admire the changes in the earth; journal about growth in a particular area

Ostara Recipe: Deviled Eggs

Ingredients

   6 hard-boiled eggs

   ¼ cup mayonnaise

   2 tablespoons mustard

   1 teaspoon brown sugar

   salt and pepper to taste

Directions:

1. Halve the hard-boiled eggs, placing the yolks in a mixing bowl. Mash yolks with a fork.

2. Add remaining ingredients. Mix well.

3. Spoon or pipe the mixture into the well of the egg whites.

4. Refrigerate for two hours. Enjoy!

Beltane (May 1–2)

The third and final of the fertility sabbats, Beltane falls on May 1, halfway between the spring equinox and summer solstice. The word derives from Old Irish, meaning "bright fire," with *Bel* coming from the ancient solar god Belenus. Beltane is also celebrated as May Day, and the Romans called it Floralia or the flower festival. But no matter what May 1 is called, it's celebrated with music, fragrance, revelry, and sex. This sabbat is associated with unions and handfasting ceremonies.

Beltane is the time when the goddess and the god join together to consummate their marriage. Lady Spring has reached her fullness and the Green Man takes her where they dance and celebrate, turning the land green once again, filling it with flowers and blooms, thus representing youth, beauty, vitality, sensuality, and health.

It's no surprise that Beltane, a celebration of birth and life, falls directly across the Wheel of the Year from Samhain, the sabbat associated with death. The two mirror one another in the ethereal realm, with Samhain opening the veil to ancestors and passed loved ones and Beltane opening the veil to fair folk and the fae. Beltane is the perfect sabbat to leaving offerings to faeries in the form of sweet breads, honey, and milk, showing them how much you appreciate the abundance provided by the land. It's also an ideal sabbat to complete love and self-love spells and for rituals that focus on prosperity and increasing of any kind, whether that be in relationships, luck, wealth, or creativity.

BELTANE CORRESPONDENCES

Colors: brown, green, pink, red, orange

Animals: bee, rabbit, frog, cow, swan, cat

Flowers: rose, foxglove (for the far), lavender, bluebells, hyacinth

Scents: honeysuckle, lavender, hyacinth, rose

Gemstones: bloodstone, amber, rose quartz, amethyst, carnelian, emerald

Herbs: lavender, yarrow, thyme, mint

Food: breads, wine, berries, honey, milk, oats, fresh greens

Ways to celebrate: make some fairy cakes; make a mini maypole; build a fire; cast a spell surrounding love, self-love, or fertility; indulge in a self-love ritual bath

Beltane Recipe: Fairy Cake

This recipe is a fun one to make with little ones. Or with anybody, really, because who doesn't love a cupcake? I love making these for Beltane with my son because they don't require much time, have only four ingredients, and taste scrumptious. Plus, what fairy wouldn't love an offering like this?

Ingredients

    1 cup softened butter (unsalted or salted)

    1 cup white sugar

    1¾ cups self-rising flour, divided

    4 eggs, beaten and divided

Instructions

1. Preheat oven to 350 degrees. Grease 24 muffin tins with butter or line with paper liners.

2. Beat butter and sugar in a large bowl with a hand mixer or in a stand mixer until light and fluffy.

3. Add half of the flour and half of the eggs. Mix until smooth.

4. Add the remaining ingredients and mix until batter is light and fluffy. Carefully spoon evenly into prepared muffin tin.

5. Bake for 10–12 minutes or until golden brown.

*Leave the light and fluffy fairy cakes as they are or add your favorite icing to the top. Be sure to share with the fae in your house and garden and repeat the following charm: *Cupcakes simple, cupcakes sweet. May you faeries enjoy this scrumptious treat!*

Litha/Midsummer (June 20–23)

Litha , also known as Midsummer or the summer solstice, celebrates the longest day of the year and the shortest night. The sun shines in the sky at its highest point of the year, marking the turn when we tip into the darker half of the Wheel of the Year. This is the time when the earth is at its most fertile and the landscape is green and full of vibrant hues. Gardens are overflowing with fresh fruit and vegetables for harvesting, butterflies and bees flitter in excitement, and birds enjoy the cooling water of birdbaths.

During this time, the goddess, now as mother, is pregnant, and the entire world is in bloom with her. This is a time of festivities of dancing and celebrating land spirits and fair folk, in addition to the magical workings for growth and fertility. Litha celebrates agriculture, the changing of the seasons, fertility and life, light and the sun, manifestation and power, and the strength and success of abundance.

Magical workings that call in the masculine power of the sun, those of inspiration and creation, those of passion and of celebrating life, are best performed during Midsummer. Because they're both springtime fertility festivals, Litha and Beltane share many customs—flower crowns, dancing around the maypole, celebrating and honoring land spirits, and participating in fertility rituals. However, while Beltane celebrates the beginning of summer and the new beginning of growth, there is a closure with Litha with the growth cycle being almost complete and soon ushering in the first harvest.

I personally love Litha because the summer is in full swing—late-night campfires with fireflies flittering in the dark sky, ice cream dates with my young son, days spent going on nature walks or in my garden with a quick run through the sprinkler to cool off. And sunflowers galore.

Litha Correspondences

Colors: red, green, blue, orange, gold

Animals: bee, cattle, horse, owl, goldfinch, wren, crab

Flowers and herbs: elderflower, mistletoe, lavender, St. John's wort, chamomile, heather

Gemstones: diamond, jade, emerald, lapis lazuli

Food: honey, mead (honey wine), berries, garden fruits and vegetables

Ways to celebrate: host a bonfire, go for a nature walk, make a floral wreath or crown, gather and dry herbs, build a fairy garden or house in your yard or in the woods

Litha Recipe: Sangria

It's the peak of summer, and who doesn't love a refreshing glass of sangria? This is the perfect time for this recipe because fruits are ripe and at their peak sweetness.

Ingredients:

- 1 green apple, cored and chopped
- 1 orange, thinly sliced and quartered
- 1 lime, thinly sliced
- ½ cup fresh berries of your choosing
- 1 bottle red wine of your choosing, depending on how sweet or dry you'd like your sangria
- ⅓ cup orange juice
- ⅓ cup brandy of your choosing

Directions:

1. Place the prepared fruit in a large pitcher. Pour the liquid ingredients in the pitcher. Stir well. Chill overnight (the longer you chill it, the better the fruit infusion).

2. Serve over ice.

3. Enjoy!

Lughnasadh/Lammas (August 1–2)

Lughnasadh (in honor of Lugh, the Celtic god of light), also known as Lammas, is a festival celebrating the grain and beginning of the harvest season. It's the first of the three harvest festivals, and an extremely important part of the early pagan's year, as a good harvest was literally the difference between life and death. Early peoples needed good harvests to survive the harsh weather conditions over the cold months ahead.

Lughnasadh is another cross-quarter day, as it marks the midpoint between the summer solstice and the autumn equinox. "Lammas" translates to "bread mass," which makes sense considering Lammas is historically the grain harvest when ancient peoples would cut the first sheaves of grain to make loaves of bread to eat in celebration of a good fall harvest.

Because this is when the god sacrifices himself to ensure the fertility of the land, many pagans create a corn dolly as a symbolic sacrifice, as well as making breads and cakes to honor the harvest. This is the time to reflect on your spiritual and mundane gains and to be grateful for what has come to fruition since the start of the year.

LUGHNASADH CORRESPONDENCES

Colors: yellow, brown, orange, gold, green

Flowers and herbs: wheat, grains, goldenrod, Queen Anne's lace, mugwort, hops, basil

Gemstones: citrine, tiger's eye, peridot, carnelian, rhodochrosite

Food: grapes, wine, bread, beer, blackberries, raspberries

Symbols: corn dollies, wheat, bread baskets, cauldron, corn

Ways to celebrate: bake home-made bread, craft a corn dolly from the husks of corn, give back to the earth by cleaning up a space in nature, go on a nature walk with family

Lughnasadh Recipe: Mini Bread Loaves

I wish I could claim this recipe as my own, but it's adapted from Moody Moons' wonderful recipe (*moodymoons.com*). I made these mini bread loaves with herbs for Lughnasadh this year, and they were an absolute hit with my family. So much so, that I'd be remiss in not including the recipe in this book.

Ingredients:

- 1 cup warm water
- 1 packet active dry yeast
- 2 teaspoons sugar
- 2½ to 3 cups all-purpose flour
- 1 teaspoon salt
- assorted dry, ground herbs of your choosing (I like to use basil, rosemary, and thyme)
- 1 teaspoon black pepper
- ½ tablespoon garlic powder
- 2 tablespoons olive oil
- fresh herbs (rosemary sprigs work well)
- 2 eggs, whites only

Directions:

1. Mix warm water with yeast and sugar. Stir thoroughly. Allow the yeast to "activate" by leaving it to bubble, about 10 minutes.

2. In a separate bowl, combine flour, salt, dry herbs, black pepper, and garlic powder.

3. Add olive oil to wet ingredients. Slowly add dry ingredients to wet until the mixture is no longer sticky. Knead the dough until it stretches.

4. Cover the dough with a clean towel. Leave it in a sunny place and allow it to rise until it doubles in size. This takes roughly an hour.

5. Preheat the oven to 450 degrees. Form dough into 5 separate balls about 4 inches in diameter. Bake 10–15 minutes.

6. While bread is baking, bring a small pot of water to boil. Fill another bowl with ice water. Dip fresh herbs in boiling water for

5–10 seconds. Then dip them in ice water. Lay them flat on paper towels and put more paper towels on top. Press with something heavy and flat.

7. About 3 minutes before the loaves are fully cooked, when they're just starting to brown, pull them out of the oven. Brush the tops with an egg white wash. Arrange the blanched and pressed herbs on top of the bread, then brush more egg whites on top to "seal" them in place.

8. Pop the bread back in the oven and let it finish browning.

9. ENJOY!

Mabon (September 21–24)

When witches are asked to name their favorite festival of the Wheel of the Year, most would not say Mabon. However, this comfy cozy witch can say with much certainty that Mabon is her favorite sabbat. Known to many as the "Witches' Thanksgiving," Mabon is the second harvest festival; it's also knows as the autumnal equinox as the day is equal parts light and dark.

As the second harvest festival, this is the time of year when farmers know how well their summer crops have performed and can often determine whether their families will have enough food to make it through winter. Because of this, Mabon is when pagans give thanks for their crop's bounty, for their animals, and for food in general.

What I like most about Mabon is the cozy feeling I get with this sabbat. Being the end of September, the days are warm but the nights turn chilly— chilly enough to eat a warm meal made out of squash, corn, apples and other fall fruits, and vegetables from the garden; bundle up in a blanket; and curl up with a good book in front of the fire pit. To me, Mabon/autumnal equinox screams hearth witchery and reminds me of the natural warmth and comfort of my practice. It also means Samhain is just around the corner, and what witch doesn't like Samhain?

The autumnal equinox is the time to thank the earth for all it has given us throughout the year and to welcome the dark months. It's also the sabbat to reflect upon the hopes and wishes made at Imbolc and Ostara and how they've manifested during the Wheel of the Year.

MABON CORRESPONDENCES

Colors: red, burgundy, yellow, purple, violet, orange, autumnal colors

Flowers and herbs: fern, marigold, milkweed, pine, sage, wheat, oats, hops, cedar, cinnamon

Animals: dog, wolf, goat, owl, stag

Food: apples, nuts, dried fruits, squash of all kinds, breads, seeds, potatoes, wine, ale, cider

Ways to celebrate: have a Mabon (Thanksgiving) feast, complete a gratitude ritual, decorate for the fall season, bake something with apples, celebrate hearth and home

❧ 🌰 ❧

Mabon Recipe: Fall Simmer Pot

This isn't a recipe for food or drink but one to help you enjoy the marvelous scents of fall throughout your entire home. Simmer pots are a wonderful way to make your house smell amazing without the artificial scents in some candles and air fresheners.

Also known as stovetop or crockpot potpourri, it's a combination of herbs, spices, and simmering water (simple, right?). The scented water evaporates and wafts through your home. Note: have fun with your ingredients. If you want more apples, add them. If you love the spicy headiness of cinnamon, then add an extra dash or two.

Ingredients:

3 cinnamon sticks

1 tablespoon pumpkin pie spice

1 orange, thinly sliced

2 red apples, thinly sliced

1 teaspoon cardamom

1 teaspoon vanilla extract

6 cups of water

Directions:

1. Place all ingredients except the water in a stovetop cauldron (pot) or slow cooker.

2. Add enough water to cover the mixture.

3. Bring water to a boil, then reduce heat to a simmer.

4. You will begin smelling the aroma in 5–10 minutes.

5. Keep an eye on the pot and add more water to replace water that has evaporated.

CHAPTER 2

In the Home

*May the blessed sun shine upon you and warm your heart
until it glows like a great peat fire—so that the stranger may come
and warm himself, also a friend.*

—IRISH BLESSING

It Begins at Home

House and hearth witchcraft begins in the home. I think that's something that really can't be argued. It is in the name, after all. The traditional *Webster* definition of "home" is this: the place where one lives permanently, especially as a member of a family or household.

But that only defines the physical space of home. Yes, home is a place where someone lives, but to me, home is so much more. It's a place of safety and comfort and protection, a place to nurture my family and a place to nurture my spirit. I tend to prefer not the definition of "home," but the meaning of *at home:* relaxed and comfortable; at ease; in harmony with the surroundings. I feel most at home in my own space—garden, home, sacred places—and in my practice.

That being said, welcome to my home.

Home of a Hearth Witch

No two witches keep the same house. Sure you may find some similarities when you really look—a depiction of a deity, crystals spread about, hidden altars or ones out in the open, an overabundance of herbs and spices, a mish-mash of glass containers and jars either empty or filled to the brim with water, dried flowers, and more.

Everyone's idea of comfort within witchcraft differs. There are, however, a few things that I find many practicing hearth witches have in common.

1. Hearth craft begins and ends in the home, particularly in the kitchen or living space. House witches make their magic in the home, and for centuries that magic has surrounded the hearth and kitchen spaces, so it's

no surprise that many practicing witches who call themselves domestic witches proclaim their power comes from home—through kitchen witchery, through gardening, through crafting and writing, and through self-care rituals that nourish mind, body, and spirit.

"Everyone's idea of comfort within witchcraft differs."

2. There is a focus on cleanliness. I'm not simply talking about decluttering and your everyday cleaning (although those are important, and we'll touch upon them later). What I'm speaking about is energetic cleanliness. Many domestic witches you meet cleanse their home on a regular basis, myself included. Any time I can pour a bit of magic into my floor wash, vacuum cleaner, and dusting habit, I do!

3. They have positive, nurturing energy. The energy that hits a person as soon as they step into a hearth witch's home is equal parts nurturing and uplifting. It's a place you want to come back to over and over again for a mug of tea or a chat around the kitchen table. There is a tangible feeling of joy and warmth in the home of a hearth witch.

4. There are subtle touches of magic. Oftentimes, when people walk into my home, their first comment is how cozy it feels. They aren't describing the aesthetic of my home but the subtle touches of magic I've added to the space. Over the years, I've found a way to add magic to my home through my color choices, in seasonal decor, in fabrics, in cleaning rituals, in blankets, books, animals, and more. Whether they know it or not, as soon as someone walks through my door (before they step on my porch, in all actuality), they're entering a sacred space that has been imbued with magic of all kinds.

5.   They have a reverence of nature and of all creatures. Witches, no matter their path, have a deep veneration for the natural world and all its inhabitants, so it's not surprising that domestic witches often find themselves outside in the garden or cuddling next to one of their pets.

For all you know, a witch may be living next door to you right now.
—Roald Dahl, *The Witches*

House Witchery throughout the Home

Have a sip of tea with me as I describe my home. You'll notice that there are pops of magic throughout in my intentional choices of color, décor, fabrics, and more. If the average *muggle* were to walk through my house, they may not realize it belongs to a witch (well, except perhaps for my book collection with the words "witch" and "witchcraft" and "pagan" in the titles). But magic, truly, is everywhere you look.

There are no tools or décor you *have* to have to have a magical home. Witchcraft is not an aesthetic. Witchcraft is a way of being and living. It's finding magic in the mundane, magic in the everyday.

Front Porch

The first thing I see when I pull up to my home is the three-foot-high (and wide) pentagram on my front porch. It's June as I'm writing this particular section, so my pentagram is currently decorated in garlands of lavender and ivy interwoven between the intersecting pieces of wood that make up the star shape. During the colder months, I adorn the five-pointed star with winter greens of pine and cedar and a sprinkling of holly and berry; in the fall, the symbol boasts leaves in autumnal hues of burnt orange, deep yellow, and burgundy.

There is a step leading to the front porch, and on either side of the step are plants of lavender and rosemary for luck and abundance for whomever chooses to enter the home. (Plus they're my favorite herbs, so you'll find them on all sides of my home!)

Your porch or doorway is the first thing people either see or walk through when they visit your home, so it's important to enchant it with positive energy and protection. Do a door wash over the threshold, plant lavender or rosemary (or pot them, if necessary) at the stoop, or enchant your doormat with a goodwill spell.

PURPLE DOOR

It's said that a purple door is the sign of a mystic or witch. For a pop of magic, paint your front door purple. If that's too much, decorate with a purple wreath or purple flowers.

Goodwill Porch Ritual

Use the following spell to enchant your porch with positivity and love and to invite only those of goodwill in your home.

You'll need:

1 small pink or white candle (a votive or tea light will do)

glass votive holder or small plate

small square of yellow fabric

glass of water with a pinch of brown sugar

1 tablespoon mixture of rosemary, lavender, and thyme

1 eight-inch piece of twine or natural fiber string

lighter or matches

Take all items to your front porch. If you live in an apartment building, take them to the hallway in front of your doorway or entrance. Put the plate and candle on the floor of your porch. Sprinkle some of the flower/herb mixture into the glass of water and pour the rest in a ring around the candle.

Light the candle and as you do so, call your guides, deities, faeries, angels, or whomever you work with for your highest good onto your porch by saying: *Guides of my highest good, I ask you to bless this porch with protection, joy, and love. Allow anyone who steps foot on this porch to do so with goodwill and intention. So be it.* Close your eyes and envision your guides greeting you there on the stoop of your home.

Continue to keep your eyes closed in meditation and when the candle has burned out, gather up the herbs and place them in the center of the piece of yellow fabric. Sprinkle some of the sweet water on the herbs and then bring the corners of the material together, encasing the herbs. Secure the fabric and the herbs with the string.

Thank your guides and then place the goodwill pouch somewhere on your porch, visible or out of sight, to bless goodwill onto whomever enters your home.

Entryway

Upon entering my house, you'll see a bench with a lantern to the left. Like candles, the lantern is a common item in magical folklore, representing the dissolving of darkness and danger and the bringing in of hope, its flame

A Note on Material and Fibers

There are touches of magic all around my home that may seem ordinary to the average person. When decorating, research the correspondences associated with the items and materials used. You'll be surprised at how many items you already possess contain magical qualities without you having to create or buy new décor. Here is a quick reference to some common fabrics, fibers, and materials and their correspondences.

- *Canvas: new beginnings, creativity, potential*
- *Cashmere: warmth, comfort*
- *Chiffon: feminine, delicacy*
- *Cotton: harvest, protection, good luck*
- *Denim: durability*
- *Felt: protection, good luck, strength, abundance*
- *Hemp: wind, vision, enlightenment*
- *Lace: sensuality, feminine*
- *Leather: protection, instinct*
- *Linen: purity, rest*
- *Satin: sensuality, love*
- *Silk: abundance, magical protection*
- *Velvet: sensuality, honor, offering*
- *Wool: renewal, hope, comfort*

symbolizing eternal life and the "light at the end of the tunnel," so to speak. Lanterns are also associated with the fae and inspire festivity, warmth, and joy in the house and home. Although there is no live flame in my lantern, I keep a timed LED candle inside that lights at night, keeping negativity at bay.

Above the bench is a large wooden basket with a cotton plant wreath inside, and if you look closely enough, peeking from behind the wreath is a

Rowan Cross or Guardian Cross made from rowan branches and red thread. Although there were an abundance of decorative wreaths I could have chosen for my entryway, I decided upon cotton because of its magical correspondences. Cotton represents simplicity, harvest, protection, and good luck—all attributes I want to bring to my comfy cozy witchy home. Overall, the decorative items are made from natural woods and materials, bringing inside the magic of nature and the outside.

Living Room/Hearth

We'll be chatting about my kitchen space and my office/indoor sacred space in two of the other chapters, so I want to touch here on the main living space in my home—the family room.

When we were looking for homes, I knew that I wanted a fireplace. Although I would have preferred a wood-burning one, I settled for a gas fireplace, which happens to be surrounded by natural stone and has a raw wooden mantle. Leaning against the stone is one of my two witch's brooms and on the ledge is a small grasshopper statue that my mother gifted us as a house-warming present. (My mother knows me well and knows the folkloric meaning of the grasshopper is abundance, good luck, and natural household harmony.)

NOTE ON THE HEARTH

For centuries, the hearth or fireplace has been a sacred meeting space for witches and non-witches alike. Fire represents action, warmth, food, and comfort. If you don't have a fireplace in your home, you can choose a dedicated space for a candle or lantern to represent your hearth.

The mantle is adorned with seasonal garland and candles that I change out depending on what sabbat season we're in. We celebrated Lughnasadh a few weeks ago, so currently I have garland made of wheat and sunflowers spread across the mantle with two yellow candles behind it.

We have a large sectional sofa and a reclining chair in the living room, each covered with many, many blankets. I do love my comfy coziness, after all! Just as I change my mantle decorations and candles with the season, I also do my best to switch out pillows and everyday items. Let's just say, I've accumulated quite a lot of décor over the past few decades.

When we think of the living room, comfort and relaxation come to mind. This is the room where I curl up on the sofa with a cup of tea in one hand, a book in the other, and a dog in my lap. Other than the kitchen/dining area, it's the room where our family gathers, passing stories around while the fire roars in the background. Like the kitchen, it's the heart of the home where nourishment and nurturing occur—my son and I cuddled together reading his favorite book series, family game nights on the Wii, or board games on the ottoman.

Office

My office and my sacred space share a room. In a few chapters, I'll detail the room as my sacred space, but for now I want to quickly chat about my office. As someone who works from home, I spend a fair amount of time at my desk. I try my hardest to not let clutter accumulate on my workspace, keeping the energy and area clear. Underneath my monitor is a small tray my son got me that says, "Mom's rock." You've read that right—possessive "Mom's" with the apostrophe because this is the tray where I keep my fluorite sphere, the stone of inspiration and a clear mind.

On the right-hand corner of my desk is a mini altar cloth (I'm talking five by six inches) that boasts a homemade room spray, an orange candle for creativity, and a round tarot/oracle card stand where I keep my writing card of the day (if I've chosen one). Behind my desk is a large shelving unit filled with witchy books of all kinds, candles, and some of my other favorite office items; the bottom shelf houses my ancestor altar with pictures and belongings of my passed loved ones. I have a fluffy pink and white blanket draped over my cushiony desk chair.

Overall, the tone of my office is cheerful, inspiring, and it smells amazing! All things that are conducive to a productive working space.

🌿 ⚱ 🌿

Office Productivity Charm

Repeat this charm to bring a bit of inspiration to your office space, whether your office is in your home, your car, a small cubicle, or your kitchen table.

May this space be free from distraction

And one filled with productivity and action.

Allow ideas and good thoughts to come to me,

So be it so. So mote it be.

Bedroom

The bedroom is reserved for rest, relaxation, and sensuality. I want the energy of the room to be free from clutter and anxiety, so I try my best to keep the bedroom space clean and tidy. Admittedly, though, I do have a chair in the corner of the room I call my "growing chair" because it tends to be the place where my husband and I dump piles of clothing. Other than the growing chair, I do keep the bedroom clean and clutter-free and stick to neutral colors.

I also make sure my bedside table is clutter-free before bed each night. I firmly believe we subconsciously take on energy while we sleep, so why would I want to sleep in a space that promotes negative energy or have my cell phone next to my head?

On my bedside table is a small tray housing a rose quartz palm stone, an amethyst cluster, and a lavender and eucalyptus candle. Once in a while, I'll keep a book on my bedside table, but because my husband goes to bed before me, I rarely read in bed for fear of keeping him up.

❧ ⚘ ❧

Doorway Blessing

When we think of doorways, we often think of the way people enter and exit a home, a restaurant, or a store. However, doorways are openings for energy and spirits, both good and bad, to enter. That's why one of the first things I do when I'm doing a full house cleanse is a magical door wash on each doorway in my home. Here's how you do it.

1. Mix two cups distilled water, two tablespoons vinegar, and twenty drops of lemon balm essential oil.

2. Dip a cloth in the mixture.

3. Wipe around your doorways while envisioning any toxic or negative energies being cleaned away.

It's as simple as that. You can also add a charm to the physical act, if you choose, by saying:

Cleanse all those who walk through this way,

This wash keeps all negativity away.

Be it so.

Everyday Magical Items

I'm sure you know by now that I love all things comfy, cozy, and witchy. My practice brings all three of those items together, and whenever I snuggle under a blanket, or catch the waft of a burning candle, or pick up my favorite book and imagine being transported to another world, I'm marrying the mundane and the magical.

As I've emphasized many times, witchcraft is not an aesthetic. Sure, we see the gorgeous witchy set-ups of our favorite social media creators, but the aesthetic does not the magic make. You can find the magic in the everyday items you already have. And you can always imbue everyday items with intention and magic.

Candle Magic

I have candles placed strategically throughout my home. Sure, there are many in my office, which doubles as my indoor sacred space, but I also have one in the kitchen, living room, bedroom, entryway, and master bathroom. I chose each candle carefully and with intention, paying attention to color correspondences and their scent profile.

For example, in my bedroom is a lavender and eucalyptus candle (lavender in color, too) that I light before bed each night. The candle in my kitchen is yellow and has a fresh citrusy orange scent. The candle in my bathroom is pink and smells of rose and lavender—perfect for any bathing/self-care rituals. Not only do the scents of the candles correspond to magic and intention, but the colors also have a direct tie to magic and intention.

Candles are also unique tools because they represent all four elements, making them potent resources for our magical practice. The wax and cotton wick represent earth. The flame represents fire. The smoke represents air. And the wax as it melts represents water. The work you do with the candle represents spirit.

When we think of candle magic, much of the power lies in the color of the candle. In fact, there is power in color magic in general. Here's a list of the most common candle colors and their correspondences.

Black—black is known to absorb and remove negativity or blockages. It's also used as protection, during releasing rituals, reverses, or unsticking stagnant situations.

White—white represents clarity, purity, and peace. If a spell calls for a specific color candle you don't have, white can always be used as a replacement.

Gray—gray represents neutrality, invisibility, hiding, and secrets. Use gray when attempting to lift curses, reverse rituals, or when undoing spells.

Brown—brown is a color associated with earth and grounding. It represents family, pets, balance, stability, and home. Use a brown candle to consecrate a new living space or when you're looking to connect with a lost beloved pet.

Red—red candles represent passion, action, courage, and determination. They're best used for magical workings involving love, courage, and sex.

Pink—pink represents affection, romance, harmony, emotional healing, and friendship. Light a pink candle when you want to bask in self-care or when you're seeking a new relationship.

Purple—related to the third eye chakra, purple represents spiritual power, intuition and wisdom, tranquility and peace, and psychic power. Light a purple candle when working with divination or calling for peace.

Yellow—yellow relates to joy, creativity, optimism, and intelligence. When you wish to bring some joy and sunlight into your life, or when you're looking for a pick-me-up, light a yellow candle.

Orange—orange represents success, inspiration, and attraction. Light and meditate with an orange candle before a job interview or when you're in search of some creativity for a new project.

Green—green represents abundance, money, prosperity, and healing. It's best to work with green candles during money or abundance spells and rituals.

Blue—blue represents healing, health, communication, dreams, and forgiveness. Meditate with a blue candle for peace, or use a blue candle for healing and forgiveness spell work.

Gold—gold represents masculine energy, the sun, and creativity and passion. Use gold candles during the sabbats that celebrate the god or during your sun energy–driven rituals.

Silver—silver represents feminine energy, the moon, and emotions. Use silver candles to honor Goddess or to use during moon rituals.

PREPARING FOR CANDLE WORKINGS

If you plan to do any magical workings with candles, there are steps you can take to hone in on your intention to get the best possible results. First, you should physically clean the candle and cleanse it from negative energy. Inspect the candle for any signs of dirt and wash it off. To energetically cleanse the candle, you can place it under the light of a full moon, dip it in water, or waft herbal smoke around it.

Next, anoint your candle with oil and dress it with herbs. Do not skip this step, as this is when you impart your energy and intention into the candle. First, select an oil that corresponds to your intention. If it's a releasing ritual, rub the candle in downward strokes. If you're doing a spell to bring or attract something to you, use upward strokes to anoint the candle. Then dress the candle by rolling it in corresponding herbs or sprinkling the herbs over the top. While anointing and dressing your candle, be sure to focus on the intention you wish to see come to fruition.

Warning: Do not anoint and dress your candle up to the wick. Stop a half inch from the top. Never leave a burning candle unattended and always have a way to put out a flame if need be.

Tip: Rather than blowing out your candle, use a candle snuffer to seal the spell.

Candle Charms to Bless Your Home

Bring bright blessings into your home by lighting the candles and saying the blessings below. Although best performed during a new moon, you can say these quick blessings at any time. Even better if you choose to do so after a good magical house cleaning.

Bedroom. Light a lavender or green candle and say, May this room be blessed with love, relaxation, and peace.

Kitchen. Light an orange or red candle and say, May this hearth be blessed with the element of fire and nourishment.

Family/living room. Light a brown candle and say, May this family room be blessed with joy and happiness as family gathers here.

Bathroom. Light a blue candle and say, May this space be blessed with cleansing and renewal energies.

Sacred Space. Light a purple candle and say, May this space be blessed with spiritual connection and enlightenment.

Garage/Carport. Light a black candle and say, May this space and vehicles be blessed with protection.

Office. Light a green candle and say, May this space be blessed with productivity and increasing abundance.

Color Magic

Although many witches choose to use color magic when working with candles, there are other ways to integrate color magic into your life in subtle, meaningful ways. Think about the colors you use to decorate your home, or the clothing you choose for the day. How can you incorporate color correspondences into your wardrobe and outfit choices? What about your makeup routine?

One of the fastest ways to incorporate color magic into your routine is through consuming it as food. Also keep in mind that when using color magic, the most important aspect of the magical working is you. We all find different meaning in colors, so when choosing colors, use what resonates with you.

The seven main chakras are energy centers in our bodies that give clues to our emotional, physical, and spiritual states of being. Each is associated with a color.

- *Red—root chakra, representing home and grounding*
- *Orange—sacral chakra, representing ambition and passion*
- *Yellow—solar plexus chakra, representing confidence and inspiration*
- *Green/Pink—heart chakra, representing emotions, love, and relationships*
- *Blue—throat chakra, representing communication and health*
- *Violet—third eye chakra, representing intuition and knowledge*
- *White—crown chakra, representing clarity and higher self*

Crystal Magic

Crystals and other stones from the earth have been part of earth-based practices for thousands of years. The first historical use of crystals came from the Sumerians, who used them in magical formulas. They were also used over five thousand years ago in ancient Chinese medicine for healing rituals. Ancient Egyptians were known to mine for crystals and used them in their jewelry, ancestor honoring and rituals, and for their metaphysical properties. It's fascinating to think that crystals are millions of years old, and one of the oldest and simplest ways to tap into the power of the earth and her history.

Crystals can take a variety of shapes, colors, and forms. Here are a few of the best crystals to have in your home to promote a comfy, cozy, and nurturing space.

Amethyst—a calming stone that aids in meditation and tranquility. Meditate with amethyst to feel more at peace or to ease a headache. Amethyst also helps in the development of intuition, spiritual awareness, and is related to the third eye chakra.

Aquamarine—not only gorgeous to look at with its tranquil blue-green appearance, aquamarine reduces fear and tension and assists in speaking your own truth.

Aventurine—commonly referred to as the "stone of opportunity," aventurine is known for its use in prosperity and abundance rituals.

Black Tourmaline—a stone commonly used for safety and protection, black tourmaline can help shield you from any negative energy nearby.

Carnelian—known best for enhancing creativity and sensuality, carnelian is a powerful stone that also soothes stomach pain and aids in digestion.

Citrine—this yellow-orange stone is one of success, confidence, and abundance. Hold on to it to raise your self-esteem or when you're in need of a boost of courage.

Clear Quartz—a power stone of healing that amplifies the earth's energy, this stone can be programmed to a specific intention and works as a substitute should you not have a particular stone for a working.

Howlite—this white and gray marbled stone helps tame anger and promotes a clear heart and mind. It's also a powerful aid in magical workings regarding insomnia or sleep disturbances.

Lapis Lazuli—related to the throat chakra, this stone assists in focus, communication, and also aids in meditation. Hold on to lapis lazuli while you meditate to help you see messages more clearly.

Moonstone—a powerful stone connected to the divine feminine, moonstone soothes emotions and encourages peace and harmony between the tangible and ethereal worlds.

Obsidian—a powerful stone of protection, obsidian is known to assist in repelling negative energies and spirits. Use it in protection rituals or hold it in your hands when you're doing any work that requires you to deal with your fears.

Peridot—this yellowish-green gemstone is symbolic of the sun and is known to invite compassion, forgiveness, and positivity into a person's life. It's known to help with sleep and was once thought to protect wearers from nightmares.

Rose Quartz—this pink-hued stone is well known for its association with love, self-care, and friendship. Its nurturing and calming energy is thought to assist in dispelling anger and confrontation.

Selenite—this opaque white form of gypsum crystal is popular for making wands and is used most frequently for purifying negative energies and activating positive ones. You can energetically cleanse other stones by touching them to selenite.

Smokey Quartz—this earthy stone is often used for protection and grounding. It brings you into the present and enhances focus.

Tiger's Eye—this crystal with gorgeous bands of a golden-yellow color is a powerful stone of stability that helps release fears and anxieties and enhances personal power and decision making.

Turquoise—a stone of healing with a sea-blue color, turquoise is known for protection, good fortune, prosperity, and hope. It also represents wisdom and tranquility.

Blanket Magic

When people think about witchcraft and of magical tools, most wouldn't think of blankets as possessing much magic. But remember, home and hearth witchery is about finding the magic in the mundane. Sure, a fuzzy, fleecy blanket is the ultimate of comfy coziness. But they're more than that. Blankets represent warmth and reassurance.

Think about what blankets represented to our ancestors of years gone by. A blanket made of animal hide and fur was the difference between surviving a difficult winter or death. Blankets correspond with the element of earth because they can ground and center. Furthermore, blankets can be used during meditation as cloaks or in workings that call in peace, calm, and comfort. And even more than that, the material with which a blanket is made carries its own magical properties.

To add an extra pop of magic to your home, you can enchant your favorite blankets by stitching a sigil onto a corner, spritzing it with a herbal spray, or even create your own blanket using knot magic, adding your will and intention to every knot.

Book and Word Magic

Nothing screams comfy cozy more than snuggling up in my favorite chair with a book in my hands. Books are magic and words are magic. Just think about how we're transported to another world through our imagination when reading. And what of words? They hold so much power. Words have the ability to build someone up or tear them down. True magic is found in the weaving of words through charms and incantations.

One of my favorite poems of all time is called *"Magic Words,"* an Inuit poem by Nalungiaq, translated by Edward Field (*aspeninstitute.org*). The poem describes a world where animals and humans can understand one another with ease, a world where the imagination mixes easily with reality and where magic is, indeed, part of the everyday. This was something that the mystical Inuits believed, and this way of thinking, like many of the myths we know today, was passed down generation to generation through oral tradition.

Writing/Journal Magic

This relates to book magic in reiterating the fact what words are magic, and words hold power. Part of my daily morning ritual is dedicating time for journaling. Sometimes I journal about something specific—like an interpretation of a card spread or reflecting on a particular event that happened during the day—but more often than not, my journaling is a steady stream of conscience.

When I'm feeling frustrated, overwhelmed, or anxious, I don't go into my journal with a solid plan of action. Instead, I let my thoughts, feelings, and emotions lead me to write. I'm always surprised at how much better I feel after getting my frustrations out on paper.

Tea Magic

Oh . . . one of my favorite comfy cozy witch pastimes is tea magic. Although I've been known to do a bit of tasseography (reading of the leaves), much of the magic, when it comes to drinking tea, are the mindful actions of preparing the leaves and water, inhaling the aromas, and tasting the herbs. I chat more about this throughout this book and even share with you some of my favorite teas that put me in a comfy, cozy, and witchy mood.

Animal Magic

Pets are a conduit to the natural world.
Whether you prefer the traditional Witch's black cat or a
wriggly puppy or something more exotic, pets give us a way
to make a connection to something more basic and honest than the lives
that humans lead.

—DEBORAH BLAKE, *EVERYDAY WITCHCRAFT*

Rosemary Guiley, author of the *Encyclopedia of Witches and Witchcraft*, tells us that during the days of the European witch hunts, familiars were said to be given to witches by the devil. They were seen as small demons and were sent to do a witch's bidding. Black cats were given a bad name during this time because they were thought to be the favored vessel for these demon inhabitations. We know now that the Church created this false narrative as a means of controlling women. (A not-so cozy topic for another time.)

Witches see cats and other animals as allies, creatures that help comfort us in times of need, and many witches and pagans have a strong connection with animals of all kinds. Most of my witchy friends tend to have animals and relate to their pets in many different ways. Some witches, like me, have pets who are here for companionship, comfort, and a good laugh once in a while; some have familiars; and others, like me again, have animals who've made their presence known as spirit guides—animals who appear during meditation and divination to give guidance, strength, and inspiration.

A bit about familiars: Familiars can take the shape of any animal but are most commonly small household pets that are spiritually connected to the witch and take part in their magical workings. Legend says they're like animal spirit guides but take on the tangible form of an animal here on earth.

Many are guardians and protectors, sent to assist their witch with magic. It's thought that because familiars are psychically connected to their person, they can communicate their thoughts and feelings to one another.

I have two animals, two fur babies, and although I don't personally call them my familiars, there is an undeniable connection between me and them. My girls sense when I've had a rough day, curling up next to me on the sofa or hopping in my lap . . . well, in all honesty, they do both those things most of the time. I also have an animal spirit guide in the form of an earth-based forest animal who has been with me in all my lives, and I also have a strong, strong love of and connection with foxes.

Animal allies are all around us—in our homes, in nature, even in our dreams—and they happily, kindly bestow their magical gifts upon us whether we realize it or not. Here are some common house animals and what they represent.

Bee: these hard workers represent collaboration, perseverance, and sweetness. When a bee appears, it's a sign of a potential new opportunity. Honor bees by not harming them and by adding honey to your teas and other baked goods.

Bird: birds represent freedom, joy, divine or ancestral messages, dreams, the air elements, and thoughts and ideas. Honor your bird friends with clean birdbaths, birdhouses for protection, and bird feeders hung in your yard or patio area.

Butterfly: representative of transformation, rebirth, magic, and imagination, butterflies go through the great transformation from caterpillar to colorful, glorious winged creature. Plant butterfly bushes to invite these beautiful winged insects to your garden and home.

Cat: a favorite of most witches, cats represent magical power, intuition, wisdom, and mystery. They also represent freedom, cleanliness, secrecy, and independence and are connected to the moon's energy.

Deer: what I believe to be one of the most beautiful creatures, deer symbolize gentleness, awareness of surroundings, a connection to earth and grounding, and mindfulness. They're also known to represent grace, kindness, luck, and good instincts. The mere presence of a deer is a sign you're being watched over by your spirit team.

Dog: although I do love cats, I am severely allergic, so the animals in my home are dogs. Dogs represent friendship, loyalty, unconditional love, playfulness, and protection. Show them love and respect, and you'll get that back tenfold.

Fish: fish represent abundance, feeling deeply, and awareness of your higher self. As creatures of the sea, they have a strong association with the water element and can assist in workings dealing with emotions.

Fox: now I couldn't *not* reference one of my favorite animals in this section. Often viewed as an animal spirit guide, the fox represents cleverness, hidden thoughts and emotions, and is an animal known to have a strong connection with the spiritual world. Symbolic of spirituality, creation, and the afterlife, foxes help seers navigate their own spirituality.

Hummingbird: unsurprisingly, hummingbirds represent sweetness, high vibrations, happiness, joy, and radiance. Honor them by hanging a hummingbird feeder outside your home. *Be sure to keep the nectar fresh by cleaning out the feeder at least once a week.*

Owl: often heard in the very early morning and late evening, an owl represents lunar energy, the divine feminine, wisdom, and the afterlife.

Owl imagery in your home or sacred space/altar invites wisdom and occult knowledge.

Now I know that deer, foxes, owls, hummingbirds, and butterflies aren't your typical house pets, but I included them because they're often seen or heard outside the home (especially if you live in a rural or suburban area as I do). Plus, they're creatures that immediately comfort and calm me, so naturally I wanted them in the book.

🌿 🥕 🌿

Pet Protection Charm

This charm can be completed to enchant your animal's collar or tags with protection and to keep them free from harm.

You'll need:

your animal's collar, tag, or a piece of clothing it wears

To perform the charm, hold your animal's collar or tag in your hands and say:

Calling all spirits and the elements four,

Hear this desire from my heart's deepest core.

Keep [name of pet] free from hurt and harm,

This is what I ask from this protective charm.

So be it so.

Once you're finished, put the collar, tag, or clothing article on your animal. If your pet doesn't wear any ornaments, you can speak the charm directly over them instead. Say the charm as many times as you'd like.

Meditation to Call in an Animal Guide

Animal spirit guides bring great peace and comfort to the lives of witches and pagans and have done so for centuries. It'll be no surprise for you to learn that they're a large part of my craft as a cozy house witch. If you have yet to meet an animal on your spirit team, complete the following meditation to call them in.

You'll need:

> 1 white candle
> lighter or matches
> journal/notebook
> writing utensil

Find a comfortable place outside or on the floor where you are alone and relaxed, and light the candle.

Close your eyes and take three deep breaths. After the third exhale, say, *"Animal guide of my highest good, show yourself to me during this meditation. Help me as I walk my path, bringing me strength, comfort, and guidance."*

Envision yourself walking along a path into the forest. Notice the plants and trees surrounding you as you walk deeper and deeper into the canopied trees. Suddenly, you hear a rustling up ahead and a clearing appears. What animal do you see? What is making those sounds? Take a step toward it and reach out your hand. Ask what message it has for you.

After you've received the message, thank your animal. Turn around and walk back on the path by which you came.

Slowly open your eyes. Take a few moments to write in your book of shadows, journal, notebook, etc., about your experience. What animal did you see? Did they have a message for you? What was the message? How did it make you feel to be in their presence? What colors, images, scents were in your meditation?

Note: If you didn't connect with an animal during this meditation, try it again and again until you do. I'd been doing meditations to connect with one of my guides for over a year before I ever saw him. Like anything good, it takes time and practice.

Mundane and Magical Housekeeping

Tess Whitehurst wrote a book titled *Magical Housekeeping* years ago, and it's one I reference time and again. In her book, Tess focuses on the magic in the home, and, like me, she is a firm believer that everything is connected. Honestly, I think most witches believe in the interconnectedness of all things—tangible or not. Everything and everyone we encounter has an energy that can easily be passed on to us.

I know how easy it is for those dishes to pile up or for that stack of mail and bills to grow. It's human nature to constantly be taking on new things, tangible or not: buying knickknacks and décor, gifts, candles, ideas, emotions. And every single thing we bring into our home has an energy connected to it, so it's up to magical practitioners to assess the energy of what we invite into our homes and do everything necessary to either cleanse that energy or change it through mundane (decluttering) and magical rituals. Sometimes a good old-fashioned trash bag does the trick.

I want to share a quick story with you before moving on. A few years ago, my mother came to visit and told me she had picked up something for me that she just couldn't resist. I was excited to see what the item was, and because my mother knows me so well, I was positive it wouldn't disappoint.

Well . . . I was wrong.

My mother pulled out of her purse a small tin of mints, the tin shaped and decorated like a Ouija board. Now, I am fully aware that just like the thick cardboard Ouija boards I grew up with, the mint tin shaped like one was a mass-produced piece of metal with a great marketing ploy. However, the negative energy I felt from the tin was absolutely tangible to me in that moment. I tossed the mints in the kitchen junk drawer so many of us have and went on with my day.

This was still during my teaching years, and when I woke up the next morning, I had developed a stye on my eye and could barely open it. I got to school, inflamed eye and all, only to realize I'd left my coffee mug on the kitchen counter. After making a fresh mug of coffee in the teacher's lounge, I promptly spilled it on my shirt. Within the first hour of the school day, two students got into a fight in my classroom—which had never happened before. That afternoon, my principal did a pop-in observation, and although it went well, it caused my anxiety to go through the roof. And on the way home, I got a call from my son's daycare that he'd fallen off a chair playing "train," had hit his head on the edge of a chalkboard, and now had a huge goose egg.

I was certain that all of those occurrences had happened because of the darn Ouija tin my mother had given me. Whether or not that was truly the reason or mere coincidence, I disposed of the tin as soon as I got home. I remember making a big production out of it by slamming the trash can lid closed once the tin was safely inside. In my mind, things would be better once I disposed of that Ouija-board tin. And things did, indeed, turn around for the rest of the week.

All of that is to say, items have energy, but we have the ability to assign energy, positive or negative, to items as well.

Item Cleansing Ritual

Use this ritual when you wish to cleanse the negative energy from an item.

You'll need:

> 1 stick incense
>
> item you wish to cleanse

1. Place the item you wish to cleanse on a clean table or hold it in your hands.

2. Light the stick of incense and hold it until a steady stream of smoke is present.

3. Wave the item through the smoke and say, *By the power of air, I cleanse this [item's name] and release and leave behind any negativity it may possess. Be it so.*

4. Use your item **as you see fit.**

INTUITIVE SHOPPING

Try this: when you're out and about and decide to pick up something that caught your eye at the store, before you purchase it, ask yourself what magical qualities the item may have. What is its color and what does that color represent? What about the material it's made from—what could that tell you about its magical qualities? And what about its energy? Hold the item in your hands, close your eyes and ask yourself how it makes you feel? Does it make you buzz with energy? Or do you feel a sense of calm and quietude rush over you when your fingers brush against it? If you get the sense something doesn't resonate with the item then place it back on the shelf and move on.

Household Energy

Just as individual items hold energy, so does our home as a whole.

Raise your hand if something like the following has ever happened to you. You wake up, excited for an event or something that will be taking place later in the day. You get out of bed and go to your kitchen to find you'd forgotten to clean up from last night's dinner. Dishes are piled high in the sink; the dishwasher still needs to be unloaded. Oh, and you notice that the floor is in need of a good mopping. All this has put you in a sour mood. Sure, your reaction to the situation can promote a negative attitude, but had you just tidied up before bed, you wouldn't have to deal with the mess now.

This has happened to me more times than I can count.

The last thing I want to do is get up in the morning and be in a funk because I have to start the day with a bunch of work. So now, every night before I head to bed, I make sure my kitchen and living space is tidy and clean. It doesn't take long to do this; five to ten minutes at most.

I start with the kitchen by wiping down the counters one final time and putting the dishes in the dishwasher. Next, I go to the living room where I fold up any blankets my family or I were using and place them on the back of the sofa. I pick the sofa pillows off the floor (my son has a tendency to throw them off the couch), place them back in their respective places, and put away any items that may be out of place—my Kindle back on its charger in the kitchen, my son's books in his playroom, my husband's socks in the hamper.

Those five minutes of decluttering save my sanity in the morning, so I wake up refreshed and ready to jump into my magical morning ritual with nothing standing in my way.

As I've said before, we're always taking in new things. I challenge you to make a habit of decluttering and cleaning your home space. This mundane type of cleaning makes way for the more magical, which we'll chat about next.

MAGICAL CLEANING

The act of cleaning your house is one that holds much power. Everything is connected, your external environment oftentimes mirroring your internal environment, so when we clean our homes, we are cleaning our spirit as well.

Cleaning is typically seen as a pretty mundane task; however, if we approach it as a way to experience more happiness, energy, protection, and abundance—using magical herbs, oils, charms, and enchantments—then the act of cleaning can transform into something truly magical. At the very least, approaching housekeeping through a magical lens will make it more fun.

Cleaning Tips and Tools

As witches, we need to make sure the cleaning products we use are good for the earth and its creatures. Sure, the occasional heavy-duty commercial cleaner is needed, but generally try to use products that are as natural and eco-friendly as possible. The following recipes for cleaning products use green alternatives to commercial products—such as baking soda, vinegar, water, and essential oils. Before we jump into those recipes, there are a few tips I want to give you.

◊   Before cleaning, approach the task as something filled with magic rather than as a mundane household chore. Reset your attitude and establish an intention before you clean. If your little one has been fighting a cold, clean with the intention of healing. If you've been a bit down in the dumps, clean with the intention of adding joy and excitement to your life. You get the gist. Simply be mindful of whatever intention it is you set while you're doing the physical act of cleaning.

◊   Make cleaning fun. Light a candle to reflect your intention for cleaning or turn on some of your favorite songs to sing and dance along to. Both of these activities work to raise the energy during your cleaning session.

◊   There is much power in using essential oils, not only for their cleaning properties but for their magical properties, too. However, essential oils are potent little potions, with many of them needing dilution before use. That said, avoid getting essential oils directly on your skin or near your eyes. Also, make sure the oils you choose are safe to use around your animal friends.

◊   Rather than letting all the grime, dirt, and negative energy build up for a big cleanse, do small cleanses more frequently. Personally, I tidy up each night before bed, vacuum twice a week, and mop once a week to avoid letting it all pile up and stress me out. Before you begin cleaning, declutter and put away things that will get in your way.

◊   Make sure you approach cleaning with a positive attitude. (I told you attitude would come up many times throughout this book.) Your attitude will influence your cleaning and the energy put into it. Try not to clean when in an angry or anxious mood, as that will translate to your space. And once you finish cleaning, say a blessing of gratitude to your home and cleaning products for helping you get the job done.

COMMON CLEANING OILS

Here are the most common essential oils for cleaning and the mundane and magical properties of each. What I love about using essential oils in my cleaning is the ability to bring the magic of nature inside. Anytime I can bring the outside in, I immediately feel cozy and connected to my craft.

Eucalyptus

Mundane use: air freshener, kills household germs

Magical use: healing, brings in fresh energy, purification, new beginnings

Lavender

Mundane use: antibacterial, fragrant

Magical use: protection, peace, sleep, purification, love/self-love

Lemon

Mundane use: antibacterial, antiviral, air freshener, degreaser

Magical use: cleansing, removing blockages, purifying, spiritual opening

Lime

Mundane use: antiviral, antiseptic, antibacterial, air freshener

Magical use: purification, joy, happiness, tranquility

Peppermint

Mundane use: antibacterial, repellent, air freshener

Magical use: protection, repelling unwanted energies, healing, peace

Pine

Mundane use: kills household germs and yeast spores

Magical use: purification, repelling negativity, abundance, success, new opportunities

Rosemary

Mundane use: antiseptic, antibacterial, bug repellent, air freshener

Magical use: protection, purification, memory, learning

Tea tree

Mundane use: hard on germs, viruses, and bacteria; insect repellent

Magical use: peace, harmony, clarifying, purifying

Wild orange

Mundane use: polisher, degreaser

Magical use: happiness, joy, success

Ylang Ylang

Mundane use: antiseptic, antifungal, antibacterial

Magical use: grounding, calm, peace

Magical Cleaning Recipes and Rituals

Witch's Broom Enchantment

A witch's broom is a sacred tool used for clearing away energetic buildup. Because of that, it should be kept separate from brooms used for mundane cleaning. Perform the following ritual on the last day of the waning moon phase (a great time for release). Store your broom, bristles always up, in a safe place.

Instructions: Sweep a circle widdershins (counterclockwise) in each room of your home. While doing so, envision a vibrant white or lavender light emanating from the bristles. While you sweep, say, *"With each circle of my witch's broom, I banish mischievous entities, lost beings, evil energies, and unwelcome guests of all kind. So mote it be!"*

Magical Floor Sweep

A great way to give our homes a spiritual cleansing is through a floor sweep. Floor sweeps can be used to either fill your space with a specific intention or to rid spaces of unwanted energies.

I typically treat my sweep as a remover of negative energies and prefer to do a floor sweep as my last act of magical cleaning after I've vacuumed, mopped, and dusted. However, your floor sweep can be designed to bring in specific energies if you intentionally set it to do so.

Ingredients:

> 1 tablespoon rosemary
>
> 1 tablespoon crushed bay leaves
>
> 1 tablespoon ginger
>
> 1 tablespoon lemon rind
>
> pinch of salt
>
> ¼ cup baking soda

Instructions:

1. Mix together the ingredients.

2. Sprinkle the herb and powder mixture on hard-surfaced floors throughout your home.

3. Using your witch's besom or broom, sweep the herbs from the back of the house to the front.

4. Envisioning those final unwanted energies leaving your home, sweep the herbs right out your front door.

5. Get them off your property by sweeping them into a dust pan, then unloading them into a trash can for removal.

6. Vacuum up any last bits of residue from the sweep.

🌿 ⚘ 🌿

Magical Floor Wash

Floor washes have been used for years by magical peoples to remove evil spirits and negative energies from their homes. Use this floor wash as part of your routine cleaning or during the releasing cycle of the moon when banishing energies are at their peak.

There are many, many ways to create a magical floor wash, but I've found the best and most time-effective way is by using the following recipe.

Ingredients:

> a bucket
> ⅓ cup white vinegar
> 20 drops essential oil

Instructions:

1. Fill your bucket with extremely hot water.

2. Add the white vinegar.

3. Add an essential oil of your choosing (use the corresponding intentions on page 70).

4. Mop your floors using the wash, envisioning negativity leaving your home with each swipe of the mop.

Carpet Refresher

I don't know about you, but with a husband, son, and two dogs, the high-traffic carpeted areas of our house can get a bit grimy over time. That said, I make this fragrant carpet refresher that cleans as well as freshens the space.

Ingredients:

½ cup cornstarch or baking soda

3 drops lavender essential oil

1 teaspoon lavender petals

1 teaspoon dried crushed sage

1 teaspoon crushed chamomile

½ teaspoon crushed bay leaf

½ teaspoon salt

Instructions:

1. Mix all ingredients in a bowl.

2. Sprinkle the mixture on a carpeted area of your choice.

3. Vacuum the area thoroughly, envisioning all impurities leaving the room.

Small Rituals for Home Protection

We've discussed the importance of cleansing our home of the buildup of negative presences and energies, but it's also important to keep those energies from entering in the first place. There are many quick ways to add pops of protective magic around your home, and I've detailed a few below.

Note: It's also a good idea to do a major protection or warding spell once a year, especially after you move to a new home.

◊ Mix together one teaspoon of salt and a quarter cup of water. Dip your finger in the solution and draw protective symbols or sigils on exterior and interior walls and doors.

◊ Sprinkle salt on all windowsills and doorways throughout your home.

◊ Write a protection charm on a piece of paper, material, or other item and keep it hidden somewhere in your home—under your doormat, under a candle, at the back of the closet.

◊ Create and bury a witch's bottle at the entrance of your home. Put protective herbs, spices, stones, cloves of garlic, salt, and a few pins or nails in the jar. Seal and bury it or hide it in a place where most people will walk upon it or cross it when entering your home.

◊ Hang a protection sachet (directions in chapter 7) near the front entrance of your home.

◊ Hang a pentacle somewhere on your front porch. You can also draw one with water on the front door or with a marker on the underside of your doormat.

◊   Keep your witch's besom/broom near your front door. Always store it with the bristles pointing up.

◊   Leave offerings for house faeries and ask for their assistance in protecting your home and all who are inside it.

◊   Bury pieces of black tourmaline at the four corners of your home. If you live in an apartment, bury them in flowerpots or simply place them in the four farthest corners of your home.

◊   Hang an evil eye charm from a window facing the front of your home.

◊   Light a black candle each morning and ask your guides to protect your home and all who are in it.

◊   Sprinkle protective herbs and spices in your food for added boosts of protection.

CHAPTER 3

In the Kitchen

The whir of a blender, a bunch of dried herbs,
Hand-written notes to be closely observed
A heady aroma that fills every room
And dancing in time to the clatter of spoons
Is a drip coffee maker, a potpourri pot,
And a gath'ring of words, flowers, stones, and what-not . . .
—"The Magical Dance" by Kalioppe

KITCHEN WITCHERY

I learned and inherited much of my kitchen skill from my grandmother, Grammy. She didn't consider herself a witch, but the way she weaved magic into her food was nothing short of magical.

When I was a child, with an apron double-tied around my petite frame, I'd stand on one of the kitchen chairs to get a good view of Grammy as she pounded out chicken, mixed up fresh dough, and pinched at herbs and spices and other ingredients. "I never really measure," she'd say with a smile while adding an extra dash of cinnamon to a pie or rosemary to a roast or mint to her famous sweet tea. And her words were true. My grandmother had the uncanny ability of knowing exactly how much basil she needed for a pesto sauce or how much flour would thicken the rue for a creamy cheese sauce or the absolute perfect amount of cayenne pepper to not overwhelm her artichoke dip. And even if *she* didn't consider herself a magical person, I always thought she was.

Whether she knew it or not, Grammy put intention and love and magic into every single thing she cooked. Her chicken parmesan reminded me of warmth, of home, of family. Her famous onion soup reminded me of the coming of springtime (I now make it for Imbolc—the first fertility sabbat). And she epitomized summer in a pie with her shoo-fly molasses goodness of sweet gooey center and perfectly browned crust. When anyone ate Grammy's food, they couldn't do anything but smile.

It wasn't the food alone that made eating at Grammy's home, eating her food, so magical; it was being with other people—nourished through food and nourished through stories, through family, through community. The kitchen of a home is a place of gathering, where people sit down together, eat a meal, and share stories. For me, part of the magic of cooking with

Grammy and eating in her kitchen was the stories and memories that came along with it.

When I work in the kitchen now, I often call on Grammy, who passed almost twelve years ago, for inspiration. And she's happy to give it. She still claims she's not a witch, but her magic lives on. Although I'd like to believe she's one of my guides (something, while I'm in meditation, she has told me *emphatically* she is not), I do know she's with me in the kitchen, helping nourish my family and watching them grow. Oh—and anytime I prepare a large meal, especially for the sabbats, to bring her closer to me I wear the very apron I wore as a ten-year-old girl in her kitchen.

> *"The kitchen of a home is a place of gathering. Food, in and of itself, is magic."*

Kitchen witchery is one of my favorite parts about being a witch. Food, in and of itself, is magic. I mean, just look at the healing properties of herbs and plants and fresh fruits and vegetables. The real magic, however, comes from the ritual of cooking and from the result of it being consumed by those you love. It's through preparing and creating dishes that we can set intentions for the food being consumed. Not only are the ingredients themselves magical, but the intent behind each ingredient and behind the person wielding those ingredients is magical, too.

The Comfy Cozy Witch's Kitchen

The kitchen and hearth space has been a large part of witchcraft for centuries. I think back to witchy folklore and fairytales—witches standing around a bubbling cauldron, bundles of dried herbs hanging from the ceiling of a small cottage, midnight margaritas in a gorgeous Victorian mansion's kitchen. Okay, maybe the last one wasn't a throwback to ancient witch lore. I had to give a nod to one of my favorite witchy films—and what a kitchen!

The kitchen and hearth spaces have been important to families for centuries as places where people gathered. Although today the kitchen in most homes is a separate room in the house, that wasn't the case for hundreds of years. Centuries ago, the "kitchen" was simply an indoor cooking fire in a hearthplace situated in the main living space of a home. Typically, it consisted of a large fireplace with a mantle. A metal pole was oftentimes positioned horizontally over the fire, and kettles and cauldrons filled with soups and other foods hung from the pole. Many people opted to place their pots directly on the hot fireplace ashes and coals. The hearth was a natural gathering location because this was a home's source of light, heat, safety, and, of course, food.

As time passed, the kitchen evolved into separate cooking spaces, including the hot kitchen, inside the home in the hearth; the cold kitchen or root cellar, an area built underneath the main house used for cold item storage; and, for wealthier families, the buttery, where beer kegs and wine were stored; and a larder, which was another type of cellar for foods that needed to stay cool. As the construction of homes evolved and technology changed the need for separate hot and cold storage, the kitchen space became separate from the rest of the house.

Although the first wood-burning stove was invented in Europe in the 1500s, it took almost two hundred years for the stove to become a fixture in kitchens. And the stovetop obviously negated the need for the hearth; however, the kitchen remained and continues to remain the heart—the hearth—of a home.

Nowadays, many modern homes have an open floor plan, and the kitchen is oftentimes conjoined to the living room and/or dining area. So whenever someone is cooking in the kitchen, it's natural for others to pass through, gather, visit while picking at food, and more.

Though kitchens have changed much over time, one thing has remained the same—the kitchen has always been a place to gather and a place for nourishment. Your witch's kitchen shouldn't make you feel anxious; rather, it should be a place where you can enjoy a hot cup of tea, cook with magic, and chat with whomever pops in. Therefore, a kitchen witch should make their space as warm, inviting, and magical as possible. And there are many ways to do just that.

Your Kitchen Altar

In the next chapter, I'll discuss in detail the witch's altar and various other types of altars, but I do want to chat a bit about a kitchen altar here. A kitchen altar is a sacred space you can come to when you're cooking to connect with home and hearth deities and guides for inspiration, to ground yourself, or to simply prepare for your kitchen magic.

In a small corner on my counter next to my Keurig machine sits my kitchen altar. Its base is a raw wood cutting board and sitting atop the board are my favorite go-to spices (cinnamon and nutmeg), a small bowl for holding a liquid offering, a yellow candle, and a representation of Hestia—Greek goddess of hearth and home. My cooking grimoire leans against the backsplash behind it. The altar takes up about twelve square inches of counter space and reminds me of the power I have and the power food has to nourish my family—physically and spiritually.

Because I include my go-to spice—cinnamon—on my altar, and I use cinnamon in my morning coffee every single day, I am in a way forced to visit my altar on a daily basis. When I do this, I'm reminded of the sacred space that is my kitchen, of the magic and intention I can put into anything I create, and it allows me to take a moment to be present, light the candle, and thank my guides and Grammy for being with me.

I love my small altar tucked away in the corner. But your altar does not have to look like mine. You may be a bit lacking on counter space, so a windowsill or small shelf would be a great space for an altar. Perhaps you've consecrated your stovetop as your sacred space and choose not to have a dedicated kitchen altar. That's perfectly fine. Or maybe you don't have an altar in your kitchen space whatsoever, but rather treat your entire kitchen as your sacred space, as your altar. Again, it's your practice, so that is up to you.

If you do choose to put together a kitchen altar, because your altar is, well, yours, you can place any items of your choosing in this space. If a passed loved one has you reminiscing about good times spent in the kitchen cooking or while eating, place a small token on your altar that represents them. Maybe a lavender- or rosemary-scented candle reminds you of the innate magic and healing in herbs—then go ahead and place that on your counter, and each time you light it you can remind yourself of the sacredness of the kitchen. Again, this is your magical comfy cozy kitchen witch space, so do with it what you will.

Kitchen Altar Items

Here are a few more suggestion of what you can put on your altar.

◊   Picture of deity or loved one associated with kitchen witchery

◊   Oracle or tarot card for inspiration

◊ Candles to bring in warmth

◊ Incense for cleansing and focus

◊ Salt for protection

◊ Herbs to bring in intention

◊ Kitchen crystals: citrine for joy and abundance, carnelian for cooking confidence, jasper or fluorite for grounding and culinary inspiration

◊ Bowl or chalice for liquid offerings

◊ Fresh flowers for inspiration

TOOLS OF A KITCHEN WITCH

Just as important as the kitchen space and ingredients are the tools used in kitchen witchery. And whether you realize it or not, your kitchen most likely has the tools needed to make magic. Although some items may feel mundane, all of our kitchen tools and utensils hold the power to wield magic, and we should treat them accordingly.

Cauldron. When most people think of the classical "witch" depicted throughout history, we envision someone bent over a bubbling cauldron tossing animal parts and other ingredients inside. (Oh—and as a side note, the whole "eye of newt" and "toe of frog" and the like were actually secret names for common plants and herbs.) All the modern witch needs is a basic stock pot or a saucepan for brewing their "potions."

Mortar and pestle. A mortar and pestle is made from a natural stone material, wood, or even metal, and is used for grinding herbs, plants, and nuts. You simply place your ingredients in the mortar and firmly press the pestle against the mortar's inner surface to crush the ingredients. I must say, there's something therapeutic in grinding plants and herbs to a fine powder.

Witch's spoon. Think of any spoon or spatula as your wand in the kitchen. Use it to direct energy and to stir intention into broths, soups, stews, or any dish you choose. Make it extra magical by etching or drawing sigils into its handle.

Cooking grimoire. Although you may already have a grimoire, you may want to consider creating one just for your kitchen witchery. Your cooking grimoire is simply a recipe book containing food-related rituals and spells, ingredient correspondences, and your cooking process.

Teapot. Although not a necessary tool of a kitchen witch, I personally love the cozy and magical sense I get anytime I pour from my teapot. You can use this to heat water or as a vessel to infuse tea into liquid. Ceramic, glass, and cast iron make the best teapots.

Witch's pantry. One of my favorite places in my kitchen is the cabinet of herbs and utensils next to my stovetop. Your witch's pantry is your cupboard filled with magical tools and ingredients. To avoid anxiety when needing to find items, keep your pantry stocked, organized, and clean.

Broom/besom. Traditionally a broom symbolized the bringing together of the masculine and feminine—the staff and the brush, respectively—and was often used in fertility festivals and rituals surrounding the growing seasons. In a witch's kitchen, the broom is used to cleanse a space of negativity by sweeping away unwanted energy.

HERB MAGIC

Of all plants used in magical workings, herbs are arguably the most common. They make powerful charms, tinctures, and infusions. They cleanse sacred spaces through burning. And they are a staple in any witch's kitchen pantry.

Witches and pagans have been using herbs in their cooking and in their magical workings since before the beginning of recorded time. Ancient Egyptians used myrrh, frankincense, fennel, and juniper in their offerings, and in addition to amulets and jewels, pharaohs were buried with a variety of herbs like thyme, lavender, cedar, and peppermint to assist in the embalming process and help them move to the next world. Healers throughout time have used herbs to treat ailments from menstrual cramps and common colds to blood diseases and headaches, and many over-the-counter remedies consumed today are created with these healing herbs.

Beyond the healing properties of herbs, however, are the magical uses of herbs. Although dozens of books have been written about herb and plant magic (my two personal favorite references being Scott Cunningham's *Encyclopedia of Herbs* and *Blackthorn's Botanical Magic* by Amy Blackthorn), I felt it fitting to give a quick rundown of common intentions and corresponding herbs as a quick reference. Much of kitchen witchery comes from the use of herbs and their magical correspondences in your recipes to create a desired outcome.

Happiness—mint, cinnamon, dandelion

Health—cinnamon, chamomile, allspice, coriander

Clarity—lemongrass, orange, lemon, marjoram

Love—vanilla, coriander, cinnamon

Abundance—basil, thyme, spearmint, dill

Protection—garlic, peppermint, basil, angelica, cinnamon

Success—saffron, rosemary, bay, thyme

Divination—mugwort, ginger

Peace—clary sage, mint, lemon balm, lavender

Luck—allspice, nutmeg, thyme, chamomile

All above intentions—salt

Tea Magic

Naturally, I couldn't write this chapter without including tea. A large part of my practice revolves around comfort (no, really?!), and something that immediately puts me in a calm, comfortable state is a cup of hot tea. Every single step of the tea-making process—choosing a tea based on my mood/intention, heating it, adding sweeteners and cream, stirring, and drinking—calms, grounds, and connects me to my practice.

Tea was first consumed in China nearly 5,000 years ago. As legend has it, in 2732 BC, Emperor Shen Nung discovered tea leaves when some accidentally blew from a bush and into his pot of hot water. So taken by the pleasant aroma and the warm feeling that overcame him as he sipped on it, he decided to spend his life studying tea.

From there, the study and use of tea spread around the world, with various teas and herbs being discovered that could soothe and heal. Tea and witchcraft have been linked for centuries due to the healing properties of tea and the history of witches as healers.

What I enjoy most about tea is its ability to make us be mindful and go inward, really thinking about who we are as witches and what our practice and craft means to us. Personally, it allows me a moment to just *be* in the moment. I carefully choose tea and herbs and the added goodies (milk, honey, etc.) depending on what I wish to accomplish or what I wish to bring to fruition. When my stomach feels a bit upset, I reach for straight peppermint tea. When I need to calm my nerves or help induce sleep, I reach for chamomile and lavender. When I want to check in with myself and simply take a moment to relax, I reach for my favorites—honey bush or red rooibos with a touch of honey and cream. And then I enjoy, oftentimes with a mindfulness ritual.

Chai Tea Recipe

Chai tea is great to sip on for luck, protection, and strength due to the magical properties of the ingredients.

Ingredients:

4 cups water

5 teaspoons black tea

½ teaspoon cardamom

½ teaspoon nutmeg

¼ teaspoon ginger

10 cloves

1 teaspoon cinnamon

1 teaspoon black pepper

milk and/or honey to taste

Directions:

1. Combine all ingredients in a pot and simmer for 10–12 minutes.

2. Allow to steep for another 5–7 minutes.

3. Strain before serving.

4. Add honey or milk to your liking.

Tea Blends for Headache, Relaxation, and Digestion

Here are a few more simple tea recipes for specific issues. Make the same way as for any loose tea.

Tea for a Headache

1 teaspoon dried catnip

1½ cups boiling water

honey to taste

Tea for Relaxation

1 teaspoon dried chamomile

1½ cups boiling water

Tea for Digestion

1 teaspoon fresh mint

1½ cups boiling water

KITCHEN RITUALS

Witches may or may not grow their own food in gardens or on farms, or hunt or raise their own animals for consumption, but they do have an interest and appreciation for the source of their sustenance. Food is treated with reverence for the magical phenomenon that it is, and all aspects of its preparation are approached as ritual, rather than as household chores.

—LISA CHAMBERLAIN, *WICCA KITCHEN WITCHERY*

Grammy was a shop-around-the-aisles kind of woman. Although she did always have a snack drawer just under the silverware drawer filled with pretzels, kettle-cooked chips, and those tiny powdered donuts I would sneak on an almost-daily basis, most of the food we made together was fresh, from scratch, and from her own farm or other local farms. And talk about gardens—Grammy had gardens galore filled with herbs of all kinds, vegetables, flowers, and fruit. She also had a vineyard where I one time had an unfortunate four-wheeling accident. But that's a story for another day.

Even though I may not have been the biggest fan of dirt, I was *always* willing to get my hands dirty in my grandmother's garden. Grammy would send me out to gather fresh flowers for the countertop, cucumbers to dunk in veggie dips, and my personal favorite—fresh mint for the famous mint sweet tea I talked about earlier in the chapter. When we created food together, we used as much as we could from the land and were grateful for all we were given.

That has carried me throughout my practice of kitchen witchery. I'm a firm believer that witches can show their appreciation for earth's bounty by using and celebrating foods in as close as they can get to their natural form. I urge you to try harkening back to the roots of your ancestors—those who hunted and gathered and planted and tended and harvested and prepared and cooked. Getting your hands dirty in soil; watching seeds sprout to seed-lings and then to full-fledged herbs, flowers, and plants; then using those very ingredients in your own cooking, all contain an element of comfy cozi-ness—and they require mindfulness.

To do these things, you are forced to be in the present moment, grounded every step of the way. I firmly believe magic happens in those mindful moments of presence and grounding, and that being grounded is the basis for

> *"Magic happens in those mindful moments of presence and grounding."*

any magical working whether in front of your altar, during a formal ritual, or in your kitchen. And being in the present makes us mindful of each ingredi-ent, its uses, and its magical properties.

In this last portion of the chapter, I'll be sharing with you a variety of bless-ings, rituals, meditations, and recipes to use in your kitchen witchery to create a comfortable and cozy space and to nourish your body, spirit, and family.

🌿 🥕 🌿

Comfy Cozy Kitchen Witchery Affirmations

Say one of the following affirmations whenever you see fit.

I nourish my body.

I only eat foods that serve me.

I treat my body with respect.

I create magic in the kitchen.

I am listening to my body.

The food I eat empowers me.

I choose to work and eat mindfully.

Small Rituals to Balance Your Witch's Kitchen

As with other areas of your home, the kitchen can oftentimes host negative energy. Just think about how many times people pass through on any given day, then think about the energy they could be putting off that gets *stuck* in your sacred cooking space. Any space that is frequented by others can hold on to unwanted energy. Below are a few short rituals for clearing negative, unwanted energies from your sacred culinary space.

◊ Clean. Wipe down your counters, appliances, and floor with a natural, essential oil-based cleaning solution.

◊ Sweep. Grab your besom or any broom you have handy and sweep. While you're doing this, imagine the unwanted energies disappearing from the space.

◊ Tidy up. A cluttered space clutters the mind and feeds on negative energy, trapping it in. Declutter, reorganize, and purge items if need be. If your space is so cluttered that it causes you stress, then you will not be doing any sort of comfy cozy kitchen witchery there.

◊ Refresh your kitchen altar. Take a few moments or even a few hours to refresh your kitchen altar. Wipe down the surface, grab a fresh altar cloth, swap out a candle, or add new correspondences.

◊ Open windows. Call on the element of air to help you clear and cleanse your kitchen space. Open all windows in your kitchen or adjoining rooms and allow that stagnant energy to escape. In fact, tell it to do just that—escape.

◊ Smoke cleanse. Cleanse your cooking space with a herbal wand. Any herbs you enjoy using in the kitchen (think dried rosemary, sage, thyme, or lavender) will work well for this space.

◊ Ask for assistance. Ask your guides, ancestors, deities, fairies—whomever you work with—to help you in cleansing your kitchen witchery space. Be sure to give them an offering and send gratitude their way for assisting you.

Kitchen Energy Cleansing Spray Recipe and Ritual

Although smoke is oftentimes used to cleanse a space, many people (and animals, for that matter) suffer from respiratory issues that can be triggered by smoke. One of the most efficient ways to cleanse a kitchen space is with a homemade herbal spray. Rosemary, lemon, and thyme have been used for centuries as cleansing agents, so the blend below is perfect for cleaning your kitchen space.

Ingredients:

4 ounces distilled water

1 teaspoon witch hazel

7 drops lemon essential oil

7 drops rosemary essential oil

7 drops thyme essential oil

Instructions:

1. Combine all ingredients in a bowl and stir together.

2. Pour the ingredients into a spray bottle and shake well.

3. Before cleansing the space, be sure to move anything out of the way that you don't wish to get sprayed (open containers of food, dishes, silverware, etc.). Tidy up and put things in their proper place. Start in one area of the room and spritz the air while saying *"May my space be cleansed and ready for use."* Circle the room widdershins (counterclockwise), continuing to say the words with each spray. With each spritz, imagine the spray spreading in the air and pushing away all unwanted energies. When you've circled the entire room, you're ready to get to work.

*Note: when you're stirring or moving deosil (clockwise), you're calling in positive energy. When you're doing so widdershins, you're banishing.

Kitchen Altar Consecration Ritual

If you want a dedicated sacred altar space in your kitchen, it's never a bad idea to consecrate the space and the tools you place on the altar, and the rite is simple to do.

You'll need:

a white candle and candle holder

a small bowl

purified water (moon water works)

sea salt

dried herbs of your choosing

Light the candle on your kitchen altar space. Place the bowl on your altar and pour the water in the bowl. Sprinkle a pinch of salt and herbs in the water and stir the water clockwise.

Dip your fingers into the bowl and sprinkle the water over your altar/kitchen space while saying, *"I ask my guides, hearth deities, and ancestors to bless this space for the highest good."*

Once finished, since this is a kitchen-specific ritual, feel free to pour the remaining water down the kitchen sink drain.

Kitchen Meditation

It's easy to get distracted in the kitchen or simply get into a routine that allows your mind to wander to lists of tasks you need to accomplish, future plans, memories of the past, and more. But when you choose to work in the kitchen mindfully—truly focusing on your prepping, chopping, kneading, washing, slicing—you're able to anchor your mind and focus on what is happening in the present, noticing the smells, tastes, sights, textures of each ingredient.

This, my witchy friends, is where the magic happens. But more importantly, when you're mindful of the ingredients you choose and the recipes you use, the food you prepare will come out filled with intent and nourishment. When you cook mindfully for yourself or for the ones you love, they will take note of the care and magic you've fused into their meal.

To do the meditation, you'll need:

> your favorite fragrant herbs
>
> a warm cup of tea or coffee, made to your liking

Sit at your kitchen table or in front of your kitchen altar. Get in a comfortable position and take seven deep breaths, inhaling through your nose and out through your mouth.

You should feel more and more relaxed with each breath. After the seventh breath, grab a herb of your choice and hold it close to your face. Notice the smell of the herb. Is it sweet? Fresh? Take note of its look. Is the herb flat? Are there grooves in its stem? What colors do you see? Focus on its appearance alone. Now move to its taste. Tear a piece of the herb from its stem (if dried loose herbs, take a small piece) and taste it. What is its flavor profile? Sweet? Spicy?

Now move on to your drink. What does it smell like? Take a sip. Notice its temperature and the feel of it moving across your lips, in your mouth, and down your throat. What sensations or feelings come over you?

Once finished, write down everything you can remember about this mindful activity. This is when you can tap into your intuition. How do you see yourself using the herb(s) you chose in your cooking? Do any recipes come to mind?

Harken back to this when you're working in the kitchen. Mindfully choose your ingredients. Smell them. Taste them. Touch them. Talk to them. And allow your intuition to lead you in using them.

WORKING THROUGH EMOTIONS TO STAY COMFY AND BALANCED

You know how the saying goes—you are what you eat. I believe it's actually the opposite—you end up eating what you are, what you feel. It's easy to let our emotions get the best of us, and if we're full of negative energy, anger, jealousy, anxiety, then that can come across in our cooking. However, the motions and art of cooking can help us release some of these emotions before they get transferred into our foods, and we can use our kitchen workings to relinquish some of those overwhelming emotions and negativity.

◊ Release anger through chopping and pounding (Please be careful!). Chop that onion with vigor, and pound that chicken to a pulp (well, stop when it's at its perfect thinness). Get those emotions out before putting everything together.

◊ Ground yourself using the quick kitchen meditation or work with an ingredient that comes directly from the earth—a carrot or a potato perhaps.

◊ Shed unwanted thoughts and feelings by peeling back layers of an onion, peeling carrots or cucumbers, or washing dirt down the drain. As you do those things, imagine you're peeling away those unwanted thoughts and ideas.

◊ Quell anxiety and bring in some calm by stirring or rhythmically mixing. Envision your anxiety disappearing while stirring counterclockwise, and envision warmth and calm coming your way by stirring clockwise.

◊ Give yourself a burst of energy by kneading some bread or shaking up a salad dressing mixture. Get an added boost by turning on some music and dancing around with each shake or kneading to the beat of the bass.

RECIPES

Nourish (v): provide with the food or other substances necessary for growth, health, and good condition

Each recipe corresponds to some sort of intention, but that doesn't mean that's the intention you need to put into the food. Kitchen witchery and witchcraft is personal in nature, so put your own spin on your cooking.

Also, the recipes use ingredients as close to the earth and their natural form as possible. I do not include ingredients with added refined sugar or refined flours or artificial flavors. What you will get are foods to nourish your spirit and body, foods to keep you connected to the comforting and grounding nature of the earth.

While you're preparing and cooking the recipes here (or your own recipes in general), keep mindfulness and grounding in the forefront of your mind. The basis of any magical working is being grounded and in the present, so focusing on the ingredients and the intent behind them will help you do this. While you're stirring the pot, imagine yourself stirring whatever intention you desire into the food. When you're packing your child's lunch for school, whisper a blessing of protection and luck over their peanut butter and jelly sandwich. Don't mindlessly go through the motions. There's no magic in that!

"These recipes use ingredients as close to the earth and their natural form as possible."

So much of kitchen witchery is not about the recipes and ingredients themselves, but how you interact with them in magical, meaningful, intentional ways.

Food Blessing

Before you serve your meals, hold the food in front of you and say:

I thank you, Goddess

For the food before me.

May it provide nourishment,

love, and abundance

for all who eat it.

Savory Egg Bake

For Renewal and Growth

Ingredients:

10 large eggs

¼ cup milk

6 ounces cheddar cheese

1 cup sautéed onions and peppers

2 crushed garlic cloves

1 pound cooked ground turkey

2 teaspoons rosemary

2 teaspoons thyme

salt and pepper to taste

fresh rosemary for garnish

Directions:

1. Preheat oven to 350 degrees.

2. Whisk together all ingredients except fresh rosemary.

3. Place in a greased baking dish and bake for 55 minutes.

4. Remove from oven and garnish with rosemary sprigs before serving.

Parmesan Brussels Sprouts

For Stability, Endurance, Protection

Ingredients:

> 3 cups Brussels sprouts, cleaned, trimmed, and halved
>
> olive oil
>
> herbs of your choosing and intention
>
> salt and pepper
>
> 4 tablespoons heavy cream
>
> ¼ cup shredded parmesan cheese

Directions:

1. Preheat oven to 400 degrees.

2. Toss the Brussels sprouts in olive oil, herbs, salt, and pepper.

3. Place in a baking dish and roast for 15–20 minutes.

4. Place 1 teaspoon olive oil in pan on medium heat and transfer brussels to pan.

5. Stir in heavy cream and parmesan cheese; toss for 2 minutes.

6. Serve and enjoy.

Perfect Roasted Veggies

For Nourishment and Grounding

Ingredients:

roasting vegetables of your choosing: sweet potatoes, zucchini, yellow
squash, tomatoes, onions, peppers, broccoli, garlic, Brussels sprouts, etc.

2 tablespoons olive oil

salt and pepper to taste

Directions:

1. Preheat oven to 400 degrees.

2. Cut vegetables into half-inch pieces and toss in olive oil, salt, and pepper until lightly coated.

3. Place in a single layer on a parchment-lined baking tray.

4. Bake for 18–20 minutes (or to your desired tenderness).

Bonus: Using the herb correspondences on page 88, add herbs according to your desired intentions. If you make a large batch of these vegetables, you can use them in salads, side dishes, or in other recipes throughout the week.

Fruit and Oat Smoothie

For Health, Abundance, and Prosperity

Ingredients:

five frozen strawberries

¼ cup blueberries

½ banana

¾ cup unsweetened almond milk

¼ cup plain Greek yogurt

2 tablespoons rolled oats

pinch chia seeds *(to ward off negativity)*

ice for desired consistency

Directions:

1. Place all ingredients in a blender.

2. Mix on high, adding more ice or almond milk to achieve desired consistency.

🌿 ⚱ 🌿

Pumpkin Chocolate Muffins

For Comfort, Love, and Fertility

Ingredients:

(makes 12 muffins)

2 cups almond flour

¼ cup coconut flour

1 teaspoon baking soda

1 teaspoon pumpkin pie spice

1 teaspoon cinnamon

⅔ cup canned pumpkin

½ cup maple syrup

1 stick melted butter

2 eggs

1 teaspoon vanilla

½ to 1 cup semi-sweet and dark chocolate chips

Directions:

1. Preheat oven to 350 degrees.

2. Mix all dry ingredients together.

3. Add pumpkin, syrup, butter, eggs, and vanilla. Mix.

4. Fold in chocolate chips.

5. Place into lined muffin tins.

6. Bake 23–25 minutes, or until a toothpick inserted in the middle comes out clean.

🌿 🥕 🌿

Herby Biscuits

For whatever intention you'd like, depending on herbs

Ingredients:

1 cup almond flour

¼ cup tapioca or arrowroot flour

¼ cup coconut flour

2 tablespoons herbs of your choice

1 teaspoon sea salt

3 tablespoons softened butter

⅓ cup unsweetened applesauce

1 egg

Directions:

1. Mix dry ingredients together.

2. Add butter and mix until smooth.

3. Add applesauce and egg, blend until dough forms.

4. Roll dough into roughly 6 balls and slightly flatten.

5. Bake for 14–17 minutes.

❦ ⚶ ❦

Butternut Squash Soup

For Protection, Warding, Longevity, and Luck

Ingredients:

   1 tablespoon cooking oil

   1 yellow onion, sliced

   2–3 cloves pressed garlic

   1 butternut squash, cubed (you can find this precut in many markets)

   32 ounces vegetable broth

   salt and pepper to taste

Directions:

1. In a cauldron (or soup pot), heat 1 tablespoon cooking oil and sauté onions and garlic until translucent (5–7 minutes).

2. Add butternut squash and broth.

3. Bring all ingredients to a light boil for 20 minutes.

4. Pour into blender and mix until smooth.

5. Serve (perhaps with a herby biscuit on the side).

Glorious Greens Salad

For Health and Prosperity

Ingredients for salad:

2 cups fresh greens

¼ cup fresh vegetables of your choosing and intention

1 hard-boiled egg, sliced

1 tablespoon seeds of your choosing

1 tablespoon raisins or dried cranberries

1 tablespoon sliced almonds

1 ounce feta cheese

prepared meat of your choosing, if desired

Ingredients for dressing:

Equal parts extra virgin olive oil (herb-infused is delicious) and balsamic
   vinegar

Pepper to taste

Directions:

1. Chop greens and vegetables to desired consistency.

2. Combine with other salad ingredients.

3. Mix together oil and vinegar.

4. Pour over salad.

COMMON INGREDIENTS AND THEIR MAGICAL CORRESPONDENCES

- *Butter—peace and spirituality*
- *Cinnamon—protection, healing, power, warmth, and success*
- *Eggs—fertility, new life, creation, new beginnings, divination*
- *Milk—feminine energy, goddess power, moon magic, love, nurturing*
- *Sugar and Honey—to call in sweetness*

CHAPTER 4

In the Sacred Space

*Your sacred space is where you can find yourself
again and again.*

—JOSEPH CAMPBELL

A Note on Sacred Spaces

Before we move into this chapter and chat about altars and sacred spaces, there's something I want to address.

When I think about sacred spaces in the modern world, through social media, what I see doesn't actually sit well with me. When I pull up Instagram or the ultimate non-comfy cozy time suck that is TikTok (can you tell I have a dislike/hate relationship with the app?), the algorithm immediately shows me what it *thinks* I want to see. Typically this includes rituals, spells, altars, gardens, cottages, book recommendations, and all things witchy. Although the algorithm does, indeed, get some things right (I love the inspiration of viewing other witches' herb gardens, witchy bookshelves, and recipes), I often cringe when I see the ultra-curated, over-the-top altar spaces that look staged for a photo shoot rather than a useful magical working space.

Don't get me wrong, I love seeing those gorgeous aesthetics, but I have to admit my own altar and sacred spaces rarely look picture perfect, and most of my witchy friends' altars don't look like those spaces either. In fact, I've spoken to many witches who feel that they *need* to have certain items on their altar or have their sacred spaces set up a certain way because of what they've seen on social media. But that feeling of inadequacy—that feeling of comparing yourself to another person's practice—is not conducive to a strong magical practice, especially not one that's cozy in nature and suited for a house witch.

Unfortunately, many people fall into the trap of being "witchy looking," of doing things because an aesthetic tells them so. I want to be clear—and this may ruffle some feathers—aesthetic is a way to brand, and being branded a certain way or labeled a certain thing is a symptom of modern society. I'm not looking to brand my spirituality, I am looking to experience it. And you should approach your practice this way as well.

That said, when it comes to building your practice, your sacred spaces, and your altars, you don't need to mimic the aesthetic you see on social media. You can absolutely be inspired by those gorgeous photographs and picture-perfect setups, but know that even if your spaces don't look like those perfectly curated aesthetic ones, they

> *"I'm not looking to brand my spirituality, I am looking to experience it."*

can be, and most likely are, just as, if not more, magical. So don't compare yourself to those posts of elaborate setups with gorgeous altar cloths, dripping candlewax, and a crystal ball larger than your head. Your space can be just as magical with a rock you found on a hike, a few pieces of red thread and sticks, or a tea light and a pinch of salt. Don't forget—spirituality has been and can be mundane. And hearth and home witchery is about that— stepping away from the aesthetic and embracing the magic in the mundane.

SACRED SPACES

I've always liked what Deborah Blake has to say about sacred spaces. She believes, as do I, that a sacred space begins not with the place or the items inside it, per se, but with you, your attitude toward that space, and how you set up that space to make it feel sacred and magical.

I remember one of my first apartments after graduating college. I'd taken a job teaching high school English in a small school district and needed to find a place to live. I ended up renting an apartment across town in a not-so-desirable area. I didn't have a yard, my bathroom was in disrepair, and every fall season my entryway swarmed with flying insects that would get trapped between the two entryway doors and die. I'd come home from work each day and have to suck them up with a hand-held vacuum. It was gross and kind of smelly, to say the least.

Needless to say, if one would walk into this apartment (did I mention the mildewy smell throughout?), the last thing they would think of was it being a sacred space. But to me—that apartment, with its not-so-pleasant smell and bugs and leaky faucets, was sacred because I treated it as such.

I cleaned and cleansed the four rooms constantly, I slowly replaced the bathroom fixtures as money would allow, I kept a rotation of herbs on the small kitchen counter, and I converted the spare bedroom in the basement level into an area for exercise and meditation. I hung a gorgeous moon tapestry—looking back, one I wish I'd kept—behind my bed, covering a large dent in the wall where it appeared a headboard had been, and I sprayed the house with a homemade cleansing spray of lemon balm and lavender (recipe in chapter 6) every morning.

In the cozy, albeit small, living room, I always had a candle or two burning on the coffee table and a thick purple yoga mat (one I still have to this day) rolled under the couch, ready to pull out at a moment's notice. I found the sacredness in those little pops that others may not have. This was because of the way I chose to see my home. I chose to have a positive, magical attitude about that small, smelly apartment and to see the sacred in what most people would call the mundane.

If you approach a space with that outlook—starting with your attitude— then any place can be sacred to you.

SACRED SPACES ANYWHERE

You can make your sacred space anywhere you go to for connection to self, nature, and/or a higher power. It might be where you retreat after an arduous day at work. Or it may be a small corner of your yard where you go to ground yourself and feel nature's pulse through your body. You might reserve a sacred space for spell and ritual work and use it as a place dedicated to magical workings and tools. And if you find sacred space in mindfulness and meditation, then your sacred space could be you, yourself. Something you have access to at any time.

As mentioned before, a sacred space is personal in nature and the location varies depending on who you talk to. Some people have the space for an entire room dedicated to their practice. Others turn to a small tray on the coffee table as their sacred space. My dear friend and fellow witch, Rowan, keeps his altar on a windowsill up high enough that his young witchling son can't get his hands on its contents. A person can have one dedicated sacred space, or many. In fact, I don't have just one sacred space . . . I have a few.

My largest sacred space is my entire home—inside and out. When I've been out and about, anxious and exhausted from running errands or taking my son to school or to the doctor or to tennis lessons, as soon as I spot my house on the way home, I immediately feel a sense of calm wash over me. (I think many of you know this feeling!) The mere act of seeing my house reminds me of its comfort, coziness, and connection to my practice, which to me is the ultimate item of sacredness.

Although that shift in attitude may seem like it comes from spotting my home, it actually manifests from my attitude about my home. (You remember what I said about your attitude and outlook affecting your sacred space?)

In my home, I've created a sanctuary of sorts through both the magic and the mundane, utilizing *many* spaces, nooks, and crannies, both indoors and outdoors.

MY INDOOR SACRED SPACE

Let's start with the inside of my home. The room in my house that is most sacred to me is my office. Actually, it might be the kitchen. But I guess it's also the bathroom connected to my bedroom. You see? I've created spaces of sacredness throughout my entire home.

Seriously, though, I call my entire office my indoor sacred space. In this room, I have my large working altar in the corner, my fairy altar on the windowsill, my ancestor altar on a bookshelf behind my desk, and my deity altar next to my desk. I spend time each morning in my sacred space sipping on coffee, meditating, performing a bit of self-Reiki, pulling cards, and journaling. Sometimes I sit on a comfy stool in front of my large altar, and other days I can be found sitting cross-legged on a soft, fluffy rug in front of my windowsill.

Although this room doubles as my office, when I enter it each morning, I am not walking into a working environment. I am walking into a space to connect with my practice, a space to ground myself, and a space that is sacred to me. I move right past my desk filled with notes and books, my laptop and other work-related goodies, and instead focus on my morning ritual (which I'll discuss in detail in chapter 7). Because I light candles every single morning and cleanse the space with incense at least twice a week, there is a permanent sweet smell that hits me each time I open the door to this room. A smell that immediately puts me in a good mood, starting the day off right.

Your Sacred Room

If you choose a room to use as a sacred space, there are a few things you might want to think about. How many people enter that room on a daily basis? Every person carries their energy around with them, so you want to make sure the room you choose is one infrequently visited by others.

Sometimes we can't avoid others in our space. For example, last year I homeschooled my son in my indoor sacred space, so it served as equal parts classroom, office, and sacred space. Let's just say I cleansed the space . . . *a lot.*

You'll also want to think about interruptions you might have in that space. My dog Ries is by my side, all the time. But there are moments when I need to sit in my sacred space alone, so my room has doors that shut. Now, the doors are glass-paned, so she lies on the other side and stares at me the entire time I'm in there, but I'm not constantly pushing her off my feet while I'm sprawled out on the floor writing in my journal or quietly meditating.

Another thing you'll need to consider is sound. Although I have a separate room in the house that is just mine, it's at the end of an extremely echoey hallway connected to the open living/dining/kitchen room. So if I'm in my space and my son is playing video games in the living room with his friends, I hear more about Mario, Bowser's fury, and Zelda than I'd like. I have two solutions to this—AirPods and Alexa. There's nothing wrong with a bit of technology in your sacred space. Alexa knows . . . well, everything. But the phrase she says to me more than any other is, "Now playing meditation music on Jennie's device." Asking my son to keep the volume turned down, coupled with Alexa playing my favorite calming channel, is usually enough to drown out that distraction.

The final item to consider when it comes to a room as a sacred space is how much clutter *you* can handle. I find that I, and many other witches, work best when my sacred space is clean and tidy. This doesn't mean I clean it every day. And believe me, it becomes a real mess when I'm doing spell work. But at the end of each morning ritual or any other magical working I complete in that space, I tidy and cleanse right away. Nothing puts a damper on the excitement of a sacred space than walking into a mess from the day before.

Most importantly, make your space your own. Add candles, soft blankets, a plush rug—anything to make it extra comfy cozy *for you*.

The Altar as a Sacred Space

It's thought that altars originated when items in nature, such as a rock or tree or body of water, needed to be honored and revered through the ritual of dedicating an offering to them. This was and continues to be true throughout many belief systems and religions. Just think of the offerings presented to deities and land spirits of years past. An altar is also the place where one would go when they wanted to connect to the divine.

I see an altar as a tangible representation of my practice and (just like my other sacred spaces) as a place where I can go to feel closer to spirit/goddess/ deities/ancestors/higher self/universe/source/what have you. But you do not need an altar to perform your magic. An altar is simply a space where you can raise energy, connect with your tools, and connect with your practice. This can be done with, or without, a dedicated altar. But just in case you want to learn more or would like to set up an altar of your own, I'll share a bit more.

My Altars

Throughout my house, I have a number of altars, and each one serves its own purpose. I have already discussed my small kitchen altar—the one I go to for cooking inspiration, to connect with Grammy and Hestia, to bless and enchant the food that nourishes my family. But I also have an altar in my outdoor sacred space. When I do any outdoor workings, I cover the altar with a cloth and place a candle and a small cauldron that houses incense on top.

Inside my office, I have the altar that I work with the most—my dedicated everyday/working altar. This is an old fold-down desk that I rescued from an antique shop. I love it because with a quick close of the lid, my altar can be out in the open and have its contents tucked safely away from visitors who may not appreciate all my witchy tools. On this main altar I keep my book of shadows, representations of the five elements, whichever oracle and tarot decks I'm currently working with, representations of Goddess, and correspondences to the current sabbat season—I change out candles, scents, and imagery depending on the season.

On the windowsill in the front of my sacred space is a small altar dedicated to the fae. (I'll discuss the fair folk in more detail in the next chapter.) I often go to this altar for inspiration for my writing and always have an offering to them of a small bowl of honey, a silver fairy in shimmering resin that I found at a metaphysical fair years ago, and one of my many faery oracle card decks. I also keep a small faery besom, clear quartz, rose quartz, and amethyst on this mini altar.

I have an ancestor altar just behind my desk with photographs of passed loved ones—both sets of grandparents and a great-great aunt and uncle who contacted me through a Ouija board when I was eleven years old. (That's a story for another day, but if you really want to hear more, I did a podcast episode on it!) I also include a tablecloth that belonged to my grandmother and a few of my grandfather's coins.

Finally is my deity altar. This is where I leave offerings, correspondences, and have visual representations of Goddess. Because I work closely with Artemis, this altar typically has items that are representative of her—a gorgeous

Artemis print, deer and fox statues made from wood, an amethyst, a crescent moon calcite, and some dried herbs and bark. If I begin working with the energy of another deity, I'll place representations of them on this small altar as well, but it remains an altar for Artemis probably 350 days of the year.

Types of Altars

As you can see, I don't have just one altar. And there are many, many witches who choose to have multiple altars around their homes. Each altar serves a different purpose.

EVERYDAY/WORKING ALTAR

This is the altar you visit each and every day to connect to your practice. Many witches keep this altar out in the open and in a main room so that it's visible and easy to access. If your practice is private or you're still working from inside the broom closet, then this doesn't apply. This is also the altar you may choose to "dress up" according to sabbat seasons. Of course, you may have a separate sabbat altar as well.

As I mentioned before, this altar can be dressed (decorated/set up) any way you like, and it can be as big or as small as you want. My everyday altar is the fold-down antique desk I told you about, my good friend Rowan's is a windowsill out of reach of his son, and my other friend Melissa keeps her everyday altar on a tray that she can move around the house with her (although it's typically in front of a large window that overlooks acres of reserved wild land).

ANCESTOR ALTAR

An ancestor altar is the one you go to any time you'd like to connect with a passed loved one, complete ancestral healing work, or leave offerings for your ancestors. It can include pictures of passed loved ones, items that once belonged to them, or anything that reminds you of them—even a scent that is closely tied to a memory of our loved ones.

Although my ancestor altar is up all year, I work with it the most around Mabon and Samhain—the times of the year when the veil is at its thinnest and it's easiest to connected to ancestors. Some people keep their ancestor altar up all year while others choose to set it up just when they're performing ancestral workings.

SELF-CARE/SELF-LOVE ALTAR

I am constantly working on my own self-care, self-worth, and confidence, and I've found the best way to do this is through self-care rituals (chapter 6) and through checking in with my beauty altar. (Yes, I call it my beauty altar. Don't laugh.) It's a tray roughly four by six inches that sits on my bathroom vanity and houses a white candle, a rose quartz palm stone, and organic lavender essential oil. When I look at it, I'm reminded of my outer and inner beauty and to move through the day with confidence in knowing I am beautiful.

If you choose to have an altar such as this, place it near a mirror and dress it with rose quartz, amethyst, essential oils you use frequently (lavender and rose are two of my favorites), and candles with a scent that makes you smile.

DEITY ALTAR

I understand that not everyone chooses to work with or honor deity; however, if you're one who does, contemplate a dedicated altar to your patron/ matron deity. This is a space you can visit when you're looking for guidance from your deities, wish to honor them with an offering, or simply want to chat with them and tell them about your day. Place corresponding food, herbs, colors, and statue representations on this altar to connect to that particular god or goddess's energy.

FAIRY ALTAR

I'm well aware that not many witches choose to have an altar dedicated to the fae, but I have two separate fairy altars. One in my indoor sacred space's windowsill and one in the southwest corner of my garden. To better honor and connect with the fae, put out a honey or milk offering, fresh flowers (foxglove is best if you have access to it), and shiny gemstones and crystals. The fae also enjoy any offerings you collect in nature, such as acorns, hag stones, and fallen leaves.

TRAVELING ALTAR

A traveling altar is exactly what it sounds like. It's a small altar (pocket-sized, even) you can take with you wherever you go—the grocery store, a friend's house, vacation, or a retreat in the woods. My travel altar fits in a zippered pouch and includes a folded-up nine-by-nine-inch square altar cloth, a black candle and a white candle, a lighter, a clear quartz crystal, a tiny pinecone, a small jar of black witch's salt, and one of my mini tarot or oracle card decks. When I travel, I simply unfold the cloth, place the items on top, light my candles, and connect with my guides and energy using card pulls.

Altar Cleansing Ritual

I like to cleanse my altar space a minimum of eight times a year, typically as I'm dressing it for the various sabbat seasons. However, before I go about dressing and decorating my altar(s), I always take time to cleanse the space. Here is the quick altar cleansing ritual I complete at the turn of each wheel.

You'll need:

> your altar space
>
> a cleaning cloth
>
> a stick of your favorite incense
>
> the tools, décor, and dressings you'll be placing on your altar

1. Light your chosen incense and wait until its fragrance has wafted throughout your space.

2. Take the cleaning cloth and dust and wipe down your altar space, envisioning that you're wiping away any stale energy and negativity that may be hanging around.

3. Lift the incense stick and wave it across your altar space and around all the items about to be placed on it. Say, *"May the power of fire and air cleanse and prepare this space for magical workings."*

4. Place the incense back in its holder. Dress your altar as you see fit.

Altar Tools

As I mentioned at the start of this chapter, you do not *need* any of the tools listed below for your altar. The most important tools are you, your intention, and a willingness to work. I add that last part because it takes more than setting an intention or using a tool for something to come to fruition. You need your positive attitude and a willingness to work. After all, as I write this, I have every intention of finishing this book before my deadline in two months, but I need to do the work to make my intention come to fruition.

I digress . . . which you know I tend to do sometimes.

If you choose to have an altar and supplement your practice with altar tools, here are the most common tools and their uses.

Altar cloth—an altar cloth is a piece of cloth or material (typically made out of a natural fiber) that protects the working surface of your altar. It can be a solid color or decorative in nature with prints and patterns. I change out my altar cloth depending on the season or depending on what type of working I am performing.

Athame—traditionally, the athame is a double-edged dagger with a black handle. It's used to direct energy, to sever energetic ties, carve symbols and characters in candles, and to cast circles for ritual. It represents the element of fire or air.

Bell—bells represent air and are found on many altars. Bells are used to create positive vibrations and as a cleansing tool. Many witches use them to signal the beginning and ending of a ritual. The bell on my altar belonged to my nana, so there is a sentimental as well as practical value to this tool for me.

Besom—a besom is a witch's broom, used for sweeping away negativity, cleansing a space, or for decoration. Many witches, including yours truly, have a mini altar besom used for cleansing. I sweep my altar besom across my altar's surface before and after magical workings or whenever I see fit.

Book of shadows—I describe a book of shadows as a magical journal. It's where many keep a record of their ritual workings, make daily observations, track the moon cycle, and more.

Burning vessel—a burning vessel is a pot of some sort that can withstand flame and heat. Many are made from cast iron, granite, abalone, or soapstone and are used for rituals that use herbs, incense, and anything else that may need to be burned in a protected, safe way. I have a small cast iron cauldron on my altar for such rituals and burnings.

Candle—representing fire, the candle is one of the most common items found on an altar. Choose a color depending on the work you're doing or intention you're setting. When in doubt, a white candle can be used in place of any other color.

Chalice—representing the element of water, a chalice is a vessel used to hold a liquid for offerings.

Crystals and gemstones—not all practitioners utilize crystals, but those who do find they carry and direct vibrational energy. Ideally, crystals should be cleansed and charged before use (cleansed with water [if they aren't water soluble], with incense or herb smoke, or placed in salt, and charged with moonlight, sunlight, or on a selenite charging plate). Choose gemstones and crystals according to your intent.

Divination tools—divination tools are used to connect with your guides, higher self, or deity to gain wisdom about the past, present, and sometimes future. My favorite divination tools are my tarot and oracle cards and my pendulum. A crystal ball, scrying mirror, tasseography teacup, or runes or bones for casting are other forms of divination tools. Although I don't always keep my divination tools on my main altar, I do keep them within reach on a nearby windowsill or shelf.

Grimoire—many interchange the terms "book of shadows" and "grimoire." However, a grimoire is essentially a reference book of witchcraft that can include correspondences of herbs, colors, and elements and basic information about the cycles of the moon, deities, and correspondences. Sometimes grimoires are passed down from one generation to the next.

Pentacle—the pentacle is a five-pointed upright star surrounded by a circle. In its tangible form, it represents the element earth, but the five points of the star represent the five elements—air, fire, water, earth, and spirit. Many witches choose to keep a pentacle on their altar—one made of wood, a drawing of one, or one carved into the altar's surface—as it's a symbol of protection and magic.

Wand—a wand represents the element of fire and is used to direct energy and intention. They're traditionally made from the wood of a local tree and adorned with gemstones, sigil carvings, feathers, and other elements. My wand is made from red oak from Pennsylvania (where I live) and adorned with a clear quartz and a protection sigil that I created years ago.

Working cloth—similar to an altar cloth, a working cloth for an altar is one that you don't mind getting a bit dirty; think candle wax, ash, salt, dirt smudges, etc. I have two working cloths that I use whenever I have any workings that I know will make a mess.

A QUICK NOTE ABOUT ALTAR TOOLS AND CONSECRATION

At the end of the day, the only thing you need to perform your magic is, well, *you*. Tools are used to enhance and supplement your workings. They are *not* the magic. Sure, you can consecrate and bless tools to add an extra oomph to your spells and rituals, but they are *not* the magic. Again, it's all about *you*, your energy, and your intention.

In many modern pagan traditions, magical tools are consecrated before they're put to use in crafting. The consecration process not only cleanses and purifies the items, but it also prepares them to interact with spirit or the divine. Like any other items you cleanse, this process is especially important if you are unaware of a tool's history or who may have come in contact with it before you. Although by no means necessary, whether you do this with your tools or not is up to you.

Setting up Your Altar

There is no one way to set up your altar. If you talk to a variety of witches, I guarantee that no two witches set up their altar exactly the same way. It's important to remember that your altar is just that—yours. It's representative of you and your practice, and the items that you place on it are personal in nature.

Before I go into altar setup, I want to address something. Here I am once again coming back to the gorgeous, aesthetic altars you see all over social media platforms, altars jam-packed with candles, incense, figurines, crystals, and more. Although these altars are, indeed, beautiful, they are not a representation of all witches' altars. I might even go so far to say that they aren't representative of most witches' altars. Oftentimes, when I see these altars filled with décor and candles and other items, I wonder where there's even space for magical workings. It's important to remember that many of these aesthetic altars are staged for a pretty photo shoot. They are not the standard you should be comparing your own altar and practice to, so don't get caught up in what you think you need because of what you saw on in someone's perfectly curated post.

What I really want you to remember is this: your altar is *yours*. Yes, absolutely use some of the altar setups you see on social media for inspiration (I do this!), but don't feel as if you have to recreate them. What you place on your altar should mean something to you, and you alone.

Although it's completely up to you when organizing your altar space, I have a few tips for dressing an altar if you'd like some suggestions.

Elemental Altar Dressing

Personally, my everyday working altar changes with the seasons, but something that I include year-round are representations of the five elements: earth, air, fire, water, and spirit.

First is earth. Earth correlates to the direction of north and represents the elements of nature and the importance of grounding. Because I personally find grounding to be the basis of my magical practice, earth is an element I work with often, so I give great thought and care to what I place on my altar to represent it.

On the north side of my altar (I used the built-in compass on my phone to find the direction), I've placed two stones that my son and I found while on a walk on a nearby hiking trail a few years ago and a small pinecone sitting atop a little wooden pentacle. The pentacle represents earth, as do the natural items. Other items you can use on your altar to represent earth are salt, dirt, flowers, herbs, and corresponding gemstones.

Next is air, whose direction is east. Air represents your thoughts and knowledge and matters of the mind. On my everyday altar, I have a sprig of dried lavender and a sprig of rosemary to represent this element. I also include a brass bell that belonged to my nana in this space, and I ring it at the beginning and end of rituals and spell work. Other representations of air could be a feather, incense, and fragrant dried herbs and plants.

The element of fire represents power, creativity, inspiration, will power, and sensuality. It's also associated with releasing, purification, and transmuting negative energy. It's direction is south. An easy yet powerful representation of fire is a candle. The southern section of my altar houses a cracked glass candle holder with a black candle inside. I light this black candle every morning during my ritual work for protection.

I also have a small cast iron cauldron to represent fire (although the cauldron corresponds to all elements!). The southern section is also a great place to put your wand or athame. Even though a candle is the most popular and direct representation of fire, you can also use a small lamp, red and orange gemstones, or a picture of a phoenix or dragon to summon the power of fire.

Water sits in the west and correlates to our emotions, intuition, healing nature, divine feminine, and reflection. On my altar, to represent water, sits an abalone shell. I also have a small chalice to hold water or other liquid offerings. Other items to represent water are blue, violet, and green gemstones; sea glass; depictions of water animals and creatures; moon symbology; and any type of vessel for holding liquid.

The fifth element is spirit. Spirit embodies the coming together of all elements and represents all emotions, all physical items, and all things. It includes past, present, and future and ancestors who've moved on, as well those still in the living realm. Spirit is about the ebbs and flows of life and of the life/death/rebirth cycle. I keep a white candle on my altar at all times to represent spirit, along with whichever tarot and oracle decks I'm currently working with. Anything that reminds you of your connectedness to *all that is* can represent the element spirit.

It's important to note that although I do have a structure to my altar, the items on it are useable and serve a purpose. Try not to get caught up in what you think you need. And for whatever reason, if you get a sense an item needs to be taken off, by all means listen to your intuition and take it off.

My Outdoor Sacred Space

Another dedicated sacred space at my home is outside. I have what my husband calls "Jennie's outdoor zen den" in the backyard. I designed it with my practice in mind. It is a large mulched island at the back of our house that has an eight-foot, round paver circle in the center. I designed the paver circle specifically for rituals, mindful movement, and meditation. There are two flagstone steps leading up to the circle, and the space is surrounded by some of my favorite privacy-giving plants and trees—a weeping blue spruce, two flowering pears, three butterfly bushes, trellised ivy, lavender, and two small evergreen shrubs.

In this space you'll also find a gray stone bench that serves as an outdoor altar, a gorgeous birdbath for my flying friends, bird feeders, some twinkle lights, a crescent moon lamp that lights up at night, an owl statue, and a meditating gnome (my newest addition!). It has taken a few years to make this space what it is.

"There is something truly magical about being outside."

On cool mornings throughout the spring, summer, and fall months, I like to take my morning practice outside to this circle. In fact, as I'm writing this particular section on Midsummer Eve, I took my practice outside just this morning. I feel grounded and connected to Goddess here more than any other place, and I've found some of my best workings and spiritual breakthroughs come from sitting in this space. There is something truly magical about being outside, and we'll chat more about just that in the next chapter.

Living in rural Pennsylvania lends itself well to creating a space such as this, and I am cognizant of the fact that many people don't have the luxury of land. Many of you reading this surely live in cities, in apartments, or in a shared space that makes having an outdoor space difficult. But remember what I said earlier—sacred space is not about the physical space; it's about what you think of and make of the space you have. I'm lucky to have this space to do with as I wish, but that wasn't always the case. In the past, I have found the sacred in small spaces; even when I had no backyard at all, a windowsill that overlooked my neighbor's roof served instead.

Your Outdoor Sacred Space

If you're lucky enough to have the room for an outdoor sacred space, there are a few things to keep in mind.

First, just like your indoor space, think about any distractions you may encounter. For me, the biggest distraction is nosy neighbors. Unfortunately, when the builder constructed the home behind ours, they angled it so their back deck looks directly on my sacred space. They say hindsight is 20/20, and had I known that was the designated angle for that home (yet to be built at the time), I would have moved my sacred outdoor circle to the other side of our lot. However, I made the space work as best I could. Simple, right?

Wrong.

Over the course of a year and a half, we planted a line of arborvitae trees on the edge of our property, shielding their view of me. I added the ivy trellis for the same reason. I look forward to two years from now when the trees have grown another few feet to completely block out their view of me. Although I don't care who knows I'm practicing in my backyard, there is an element of privacy I require *during* sacred time that I prefer others not observe. So that is something you definitely want to consider when setting up your outdoor space.

If you live in a neighborhood with houses in close proximity to one another, consider shrubbery or even a fence. You can make a big project out of it by building and decorating your own fence. I've seen some gorgeous outdoor spaces with six-foot-high fences painted in bright colors and with sunflowers, stars, moons, and other esoteric and witchy imagery.

MAKING YOUR SACRED SPACES COMFY AND COZY

Obviously, your sacred space is where you'll spend a lot of time, so it's important to make it a place you *want* to come back to over and over again. You can do this by making it as welcoming and cozy as possible. Although my spaces and my practice have changed over time, I have *always* made them comfy cozy places that I want to come back to over and over again.

◊ Add a throw rug. Surprisingly enough, I found a plush, round, white rug at 5 Below, of all places, for, you guessed it, five dollars. If you follow my social media handles, you've surely seen this rug in many of my posts.

◊ Add tapestry. You can find some gorgeous wall throws, hangings, and tapestries on Etsy.

◊ Artwork. Some of my favorite witchy pieces of art come from small witch-run Etsy shops, and they adorn the walls of my sacred space.

◊ Candles. Candles immediately elicit that comfy cozy feeling. And it helps that they're so closely tied to witchy workings as well.

◊ Scent. Spritz your sacred space with a mediation or intention spray, or with a scent you simply love.

◊ Books. My sacred space reaches prime comfy cozy level due to my many books on the craft. (It's embarrassing to admit how many I've accumulated over the years.)

◊ Meditation cushion. Don't knock it till you try it. About five years ago, I invested in a butt-shaped meditation cushion, and it was one of the best purchases for my sacred space. (I now have one for my outdoor space as well.) If you've run into the problem of your feet and legs falling asleep during cross-legged meditation, a meditation cushion will be your new best friend. If I'm not comfortable during workings, I simply won't complete them. This will save your butt (and feet) from that pins-and-needles feeling.

Altar Décor for the Sabbats

As I've mentioned before, nothing makes me feel more like a cozy house witch than getting ready for the Wheel of the Year sabbat celebrations. I love the scents of pie and breads baking in the oven, the herby aroma of stews and meats wafting from the stovetop, and the fresh taste of berries straight from my garden. There is something truly magical about the sabbats—something that brings out my inner domestic goddess. Decorating my altar for the sabbat seasons is not only fun for me, but it's also a way to connect with the spirit of that particular season.

Although not a necessity, many witches choose to either decorate their everyday altars for the sabbat season or dedicate a separate altar space to these celebrations. Personally, I don't just decorate my altar depending on the sabbat season we're in, but I decorate my house as well. Go back to chapter 1 and see the correspondences associated with each sabbat. If you want even more guidance, a great resource for this is *The Book of Altars and Sacred Spaces* by Anjou Kiernan. Kiernan describes creating magical spaces in your home for ritual and intention based upon the Wheel of the Year and sabbats. That sounds right up my alley.

A Final Thought on Sacred Spaces

Some treat wherever they are at any given time as their sacred space because you don't need a particular space to find sacredness—it can truly be found anywhere you are. Anywhere you can connect to your practice, nature, spirit, etc. Sometimes a sacred space can be a moment in time—a few short seconds or minutes of meditation and mindfulness.

No matter how you classify your sacred space, it is in those moments and in those places where the magic happens—where we can sit in stillness, reflect on the goings-on of the day, and connect to our magical selves.

CHAPTER 5

The Garden and Nature

The witch knows nothing in this world is supernatural.
It is all natural.
—LAURIE CABOT

Seeing Nature through
a Child's Eyes

As I work on this chapter, I'm sitting outside while my son plays in his swing set's playhouse. He decided that today he was going to turn his playhouse into an actual home. He grabs his kid-sized broom and dustpan set and goes to work clearing out the cobwebs. Next he moves onto the floors and sweeps out dirt and dust and grass clippings.

He disappears inside our actual house and returns with an empty bin for his books and "borrows" the vase filled with lavender and roses from the kitchen table to place in the corner of his clubhouse. "To make the outside my home," he says with a smile. My heart warms. Now he rounds the corner with a gallon bag (?) and reappears with it full of water. He runs back to his house, climbs up the ladder, dumps the water into the corner, and then scrubs the floor with his plastic-bristled broom. He repeats this a few times.

"What's that for?" I ask, as he fills up his fourth bagful of water.

"Cleaning off the bird poop!" He beams.

I smile, happy he has chosen to spend the morning outside with me, rather than inside playing video games or watching the latest episode of his favorite television show (oh, he does plenty of those things, too!). In a few minutes, we'll head in for lunch, and afterward we're making a trip to the fabric store to grab some material to make into curtains for his tiny playhouse windows—all my son's design. He's already told me how he'll decorate his clubhouse . . . of the area rug he wants, the corners full of flowers, and the bookshelf to house his favorite series. While on our daily morning walk today, he expressed that he wanted to spend most of the day outside. And this witchy mom is not complaining!

To view and experience the world with this sort of wonder and creativity is something that we've lost as a society. In this digital age, many turn to television, games, or social media to disconnect,

"To view the world with wonder and creativity is something that we've lost as a society."

while completely forgetting the abundance of calm and grounding just outside our front door. It's so simple to take a moment out of our day to step outside, and it may seem mundane, but embracing the mundane outdoors—getting our feet dirty, gardening under the bright sun, scrubbing our porches and playhouses, watering our plants, filling the bird feeders, seeing the world as one of wonder and enchantment—that is at the core of comfy cozy witchcraft and of finding comfort and magic in the mundane, in the everyday view outside our windows in nature.

I look to my son to remind me of that. Nature *is* magic, and when I'm in it, I'm instantly connected to my practice. Why spend the day cooped up inside when we can experience the magic of the world outside? So I urge you to put on those shoes—go for a nature walk, take a stroll around the city block, tend to that garden, be mindful of the sounds and sights you experience, and bask in the simplistic magic of it all.

NATURE AND WITCHCRAFT

Witchcraft has been around for hundreds of years. When I think of green witchery, I think of the folk healers, the cunning folk, the wise men and wise women who simply knew what herbs and plants and flowers worked together to help cure ailments and to help people heal physically, emotionally, and spiritually. These magical peoples were aware of combinations used to increase happiness, abundance, fertility, prosperity, love, and more. They knew of the herbs that could cause harm, as well.

Green witchcraft and the history of witchcraft has, at its heart, stayed the same—the honoring of nature. Honoring the life cycle. Honoring what nature has provided. And using what she's provided in a meaningful, magical way. And you're never closer to the divine than when you're in your garden or in nature or simply breathing in outside air, connecting to Mother Earth.

Coming from a line of folk magic practitioners, healers, and spellcasters who performed their craft in a particular region (Pennsylvanian Braucherei, for me), my family has a long history in green magic. Healers of years past were people like you and me, and my grandmother and my uncle, who just knew how to work with nature and elements and had a talent for working with herbs and plants and saying the right words to heal and bring good fortune into people's lives. They also had a deep appreciation for the natural world and saw the divine in it.

One thing most pagans and witches have in common, no matter their path, is a deep respect and reverence for nature. Witchcraft is based on a kind, loving relationship with the natural world. Observing the festivals in the Wheel of the Year is celebrating the earth in all her phases. Going on nature walks and observing the birds and butterflies and new growth brings a happiness and calm to most witches. Tending to a growing garden, whether from seed or not, and then celebrating that garden's harvest connects us to our local lands. Being kind to our animal friends connects us to Mother Earth's creatures. And leaving offerings for land spirits and the fae puts us in touch with some of the oldest forms of natural magic out there.

For me, going into nature immediately calms me, and I know that spending time in nature is a large way that many witches deal with the difficult goings-on of life—a way to find some comfy coziness. Personally, I go to the woods, I go to my outdoor sacred space, I stare at the moon, at the sky, at my garden when I'm mulling over a particular problem. One of my favorite places to go is a local state forest about two miles from my house. There's a three-mile trail I like to hike, and on that trail I take comfort in the trickling stream that runs alongside it, a cute stone cottage (looks like the perfect witch's cottage), and bluebirds galore flying across the path (a sign that Grammy is near). Oh, and I can't forget the deer I've encountered, as well as the many small forest critters that scuttle through the leaves.

When I feel the urge to be immersed in nature, I take the short drive to this place. Some of my best thinking occurs in those woods. In fact, that is the place I went when asking for guidance for this book. I marvel at the changing of the seasons—the bold colors in fall, the glistening branches in winter, the violets peeking through the brown in spring, and the lush grasses and scents of onion in the summer. Oh how I love the smell of onion grass. And the simple act of writing about these places immediately soothes me.

When we first moved to our home in northeast Pennsylvania, I remember telling my husband that the air feels magical. Truly, it's an intangible sense of magic. My son talks about the fairies he's seen in these very woods and in our own backyard, reminding me that we're in the right place.

Let's take a look at how nature fuels me for the day, and perhaps you'll get some inspiration from it.

My Time Outdoors

Join me for a morning outside. Most mornings (weather permitting), I drink my morning coffee on the back porch and take in the landscape. Although I live in a neighborhood, I've created, to my best ability, a sanctuary of sorts. I look across the patio and over my rose bushes to the garden in the northeast corner. I look to the west and to my outdoor sacred space (which I discussed in detail in the last chapter), observing the goldfinches and bluebirds flying in and out of the birdhouses. I watch as the mourning doves splash around in the birdbath and smile at the twin birds chasing one another around my son's play set.

Next I go for a little nature stroll around my house. I start with the garden, weaving in and out between the beds and bushes, then take a seat in the corner on a wrought-iron chair, its back made of twisting metal vines. There I sip on my coffee and talk to my plant babies. (If you don't talk to your plants, now is a great time to begin!) After a while, I get up and wind through the raised beds and between blueberry bushes, plucking off a ripe berry and popping it in my mouth. Although it's a simple walk through my garden, it evokes a feeling of ease and grounding within. And you'll hear me say it again and again—grounding is the basis for all magical working. And what better way to become grounded than connecting with Mother Nature in your own backyard?

After my garden stroll, I move past my son's play set to the paver circle in my outdoor sacred space. What makes the morning extra magical is the sun peering over the house and shining directly down onto this space. I take a seat on the cement bench behind the circle, sip on my coffee, and then close my eyes. I inhale a few deep breaths while listening to the sounds around me—the birds, the bees, the wind rustling through my flowering pear trees, and even a few cars passing by. Sometimes, if I'm out early enough, I catch the hooting of an owl in a tree across the street.

I find this daily connection to nature not only grounds me, but it sets my tone for the day, very similar to how my morning ritual does. As I mentioned before, we've taken steps away from nature. And although there is merit in keeping pace with the ever-changing modern world of work and technology, if we make time to connect with nature, to her cycles, to the seasons, we can maintain better balance in the everyday. Truly, it only takes a few mindful moments to reconnect, to breathe, to ground, to find the comfy cozy magic in the outdoors.

If you live in a space without a yard, you can do this by simply stepping onto a porch or opening a window to hear the sounds from outside. Even if you're in the city and hear honking horns and nearby traffic when you open your window, then take in the feel of the air kissing your cheeks or the pigeon landing on the stoop across the street. Nature is all around you whether you realize it or not, whether you live in a rural area or in a large metropolis. If only we look, we will find it.

MAGICAL WAYS TO CONNECT WITH NATURE

Because witchcraft is a nature-based belief system, it's important to take the time to connect with the outside. And because there is so much serenity and peace in the simple act of being outside, it's no surprise that this comfy cozy witch spends time outside as much as she can.

Try taking a few moments each day to make an intentional connection with nature. It won't take long, and you won't need to get in your car and drive anywhere (unless you have the time and means to do so).

◊ Watch a thunderstorm roll in.

◊ Take a nature walk around your neighborhood.

◊ Take off your shoes and put your feet in the dirt, the grass, the sand.

◊ Literally hug a tree.

◊ Take a hike in a local forest or park.

◊ Make use of the seasons. Play in the leaves in the fall. Play in the snow in the winter. Play in the rain in the spring. And play in the sun in the summer.

◊ Open your window and let fresh air in.

◊ Connect with water through an ocean, stream, or pond.

◊ Go stargazing with your family (or alone).

My Garden

My garden is simple yet full of magic. I have four raised beds roughly four by five feet, which gives me eighty square feet of planting space. One box is dedicated to my herbs—basil, rosemary, spearmint (potted in the corner, as mint spreads like wildfire), thyme, and cilantro—all herbs I use throughout the year in my cooking. Another box is for my tomatoes and peppers, another for my cucumbers and lettuce, and the final box contains my sweet potatoes and zucchini. Although the latter two share a box, next year I'll be separating them because the squash took over.

In the southwest corner of the garden is a space dedicated to the fair folk (which you'll read about very soon) and has a fairy statue, birdbath, and a looming foxglove. Just outside the boxes on the east, you'll find two blueberry bushes. The northwest corner houses a wrought-iron bistro set, and I have a compass and gnome statue in the southeast corner.

The entire garden area is enclosed by a wooden fence my husband and I built at the beginning of last summer, and we placed pea gravel throughout the entire space, weaving around the boxes and stepping stones I've placed to make an area for walking meditation.

Overall, I like to keep my garden simple, growing foods that I use on a regular basis throughout the summer and fall months. To ensure good growth and a bountiful harvest, I enchant my garden space through a variety of small spells and rituals, some of which I've included in this chapter—obsidian in each corner for protection, citrine in the corners of the individual beds, and quartz in the soil when planting bushes and trees. However, I will say, the ground in my area is *full* of quartz. In fact, a two-thousand-pound piece of solid quartz that came from our property now sits in one of the back mulch beds.

Gardens in a Small Space

Many witches who dwell in apartments or homes that have small outdoor spaces can still create and maintain a witch's garden. The size of your space does not matter. You can do absolutely magical things with a baker's rack, grow lamps, and leftover cottage cheese containers. (Any containers of your choosing, really.)

As I mentioned earlier, when I lived in a small apartment years back that had absolutely no green space, my witch's garden was a small windowsill in my living room/kitchen area. Although I had room for only a tomato plant and some herbs, I felt connected to my green witchery nevertheless. Remember, small space or large, it's your attitude about that space and the magic within it that matters most.

In a Small Space? Try These Tips

Use those corners. A great place to house your plants is in the corner of a room. Sure, you can place a plant stand in the corner, but make use of the ceiling as well. Fasten hanging pots or macramé pot holders onto hooks and you have yourself a hanging garden. Just be sure to use pots that can hold their water or that could make quite the mess.

Join a gardening co-op. Even if you don't have the space in your apartment, you can still find green space in the city. Research local gardening co-ops and shared green spaces. For a minimal fee, and weekly/monthly dedication of your time, you can share a green space and its abundance with others. You may even meet a fellow green witch or two in the process.

Create a balcony garden. You can turn your entire balcony into a lush garden space by using raised flower/gardening beds. Utilize hanging baskets and pots filled with flowers, vegetables, and herbs.

Setting up a Witch's Garden

I start my garden in very early spring. In fact, I begin planning the layout of my garden just after Imbolc when the stirrings of spring are beginning underground. I've found that many of us who follow pagan/witch/earth-based spiritual practices begin the garden planning process then, although I've been known to procrastinate, too, so don't worry if you begin planning later.

Closer to Ostara is the time when new life is sprouting from seed, and the act of planting is ritual and magical in and of itself. So many witches love the planting season because it's connected to us and our practice. To cultivate something in the soil, to see it sprout, to watch it bloom is to watch magic unfold right in front of us.

Below are some suggestions for setting up your own garden.

Elemental Garden

An elemental garden is one based on the four elements. I've seen many elemental gardens take the shape of a pentacle. In them there are five sections. One represents air, one water, one earth, one fire, and one spirit. Most of the times I've seen these gardens, they're more or less aligned with the elements' directions as well. Air in the east. Earth in the north. Water in the west. Fire in the south.

To set up an elemental garden, research the correspondences to some of your favorite herbs, vegetables, and flowers. Each one will have a specific elemental/directional correspondence, so plant them accordingly. Of course, you can also choose to place the plants or herbs wherever you like.

Lunar Garden

A lunar garden is another option, especially for those who work with the moon and her energy. In fact, you can grow plants and flowers that bloom at night. Cultivating a moon garden is a great way to get in touch with nature and honor the moon and her cycles, and it provides a gorgeous backdrop for moonlit outdoor rituals.

Deity Garden

Many plants are associated with specific deities, so another option for a magical garden is to dedicate a space to a particular deity you work with. When I think of my home and hearth and plants and kitchen witchery, I always think of Hestia and Brigid. Obviously, Gaia would connect to a magical garden space as well. Research herbs and plants that correspond to a particular deity, cultivate them in that space, and then take your deity work to that garden space.

Herb Tea Garden

What witch doesn't love a garden dedicated to tea herbs? And just think about how satisfying it would be to drink a freshly steeped mug of tea using herbs you've harvested from your own backyard. Growing herbs for tea is surprisingly simple, and you can do it in a space of any size.

Many herbs, such as rosemary, sage, and thyme, are not only delicious but also pretty easy to maintain, as they are low maintenance. Although there is an abundance of herbs that make excellent teas, I've included some of the best (in my opinion) below. Like all recipes using herbs, please make sure you're not allergic to any of them and that they don't react with any medications you may be taking.

Calendula. Calendula is a natural anti-inflammatory and is great for soothing a sore throat.

Magical uses: protection, spiritual enhancement, good luck, healing

Catnip. A favorite of humans and feline friends alike, catnip is earthy and minty and is consumed to help promote relaxation and reduce anxiety.

Magical uses: beauty, relationships, happiness, abundance

Chamomile. A perennial favorite of tea drinkers, chamomile is the perfect bedtime tea, as it promotes a good night's sleep and assists in cases of insomnia. (Unfortunately, I have a slight allergy to chamomile.)

Magical uses: purification, protection, sleep, meditation

Fennel. This tea has a slightly bitter, licorice taste and is a powerful aid for digestion and painful menstrual cramps.

Magical uses: courage, divination, cleansing, strength, energy

Hibiscus. This herb is fruity yet tart and aids in digestion, and a few studies have shown that it helps lower blood pressure. Note: there are ornamental varieties of hibiscus, so if you want to grow it, choose a variety that is edible.

Magical uses: relaxation, dreamwork, love, communication

Lemon balm. This citrusy yet mint-tasting herb makes a refreshing herbal tea. It's known for its stress-reduction ability and can help calm your mind from anxiety and worries.

Magical uses: prosperity, healing, happiness, memory, easing anxiety

Mint. I can't write about herbal teas without mentioning one of my favorites—mint. There are many, many varieties of mint with varying flavor profiles. Mint can soothe a sore throat, aid in digestion, and improve sleep.

Magical uses: psychic ability, abundance, protection

Mugwort. Teas made from this herb are known to promote circulation and stimulate the stomach; it is also known for its sedative qualities. Note: consult with your medical provider before using mugwort in your teas.

Magical uses: dreamwork, psychic work, protection

Rose. You can use either rose petals or rosehips to make a lovely floral-flavored tea packed with vitamin C, calcium, and zinc.

Magical uses: love, self-love, healing, confidence

Flower Garden

If you live in an area with limited space to grow vegetables or you simply don't have the time to spend pruning and tending to a garden of vegetables, you might consider creating a flower garden. This can be done in as big or as small a space as you like—backyard, patio, porch, or pots of flowers on a windowsill. Enchant your flowers with abundance and growth by embedding small citrine crystals in the soil.

Garden Growth Charm

Use this charm at the beginning of the growing season to ensure the successful growth and harvest of your plants, herbs, and vegetables.

You'll need:

> your garden
>
> 3 tablespoons of water charged in the sun (set in the sun to
>> soak up its energy)
>
> 4 citrine crystals

Stand over your garden, indoor garden, or flowerpots (wherever you house your plants). Dip your fingers in the sun-charged water and sprinkle it over the top your plants while saying, *"May you grow quickly, healthily, and abundantly."* Repeat those words as you plant the citrine in the soil surrounding the plants. Once finished say, *"Be it so."*

Note: If there are water or gemstones left over, seal them in a container and place them at the entrance of your garden space. Each time you introduce a new plant to your garden, simply unscrew the lid, sprinkle citrine-infused sun water on it, and repeat the charm above.

Fae/Fairies/Fair Folk

I can't talk about outdoor garden spaces without at least mentioning the fair folk, fae, fairies, what have you. (I use the spellings "fairy," "fae," "faery," and "faerie" interchangeably throughout the book, and to me they all have the same meaning.) As you know, much of my life as a witch is calm, comforting, and nurturing in nature, so it's no surprise I find working with the fae a comfy part of my practice.

Not only do I enjoy reading about the fair folk (I have no less than a dozen books on the fae and their history and folklore in my collection) and find the simple action of reading as a way to connect with them, but also the act of leaving them offerings and working with them in my home, kitchen, and garden is comforting to me as well.

There is much debate over what fairies are, and you will get multiple definitions from pretty much any practitioner of magic. The Greek poet Homer, W. B. Yeats, Robert Graves, the poet Walter de la Mare, and many of the most learned practitioners and students of the fairy magical arts—all have many varying thoughts on defining and working with fairies. Some say to steer clear of working with the fae at all costs, as they're mischievous and cause all kinds of havoc. Others say to tread lightly when working with the fae. While others say you may openly work with the fae whenever you wish—a no-strings-attached approach.

> *"As some of the most ancient land spirits, the fae are protectors of garden, home, and hearth."*

When most people think of fairies, their minds go to the Disneyesque Tinkerbell-type of magical creature—tiny and demure with glittering wings and fairy dust trailing behind them. But to me, the fae are some of the most ancient land spirits out there, taking on many shapes and sizes. I see them as protectors and keepers of nature that live on a different, magical plane from us, a plane accessed through liminal spaces—wells, natural bodies of water, gardens, caves, hag stones, and more. They're also protectors of garden, home, and hearth. The fair folk I've encountered have been nothing less than kind to me, but I do make sure to treat them with respect and leave offerings, which I'll chat about in a bit.

The word "faery" or "faerie" is Middle French, from the word *fee,* which stems from the late Latin *fata,* meaning the goddess of fate. In Middle English, *"faery"* has three meanings: enchantment, a land where enchanted beings lived, and the inhabitants of such a place. According to Sirona Knight, author of *Druids, Faeries, and Wiccan Rituals,* one of the most current definitions of "faery" is a mythical being of folklore and romance that has human form and magical power.

Although you'll find stores of faeries in cultures all across the globe, some of the most popular tales and depictions come from Celtic cultures and mythologies—the supernatural race of Sidhe (pronounced *shee*) in Ireland and the Tylwyth Teg in Welsh mythos. Many scholars agree that the fae date back centuries and are believed to have been in contact with humans for thousands of years, even inhabiting the British Isles as long ago as the Neolithic period.

Though the fair folk aren't as pronounced in America where I live, it doesn't mean they're not present and haven't been for centuries. They are, after all, land spirits, and even if America hasn't been inhabited by mortals as long as other places, the fae have always been present as long as grass and trees and flowers and water have been around—they are the sacred, magical presences that bring nature to life.

Obviously, this is a simple overview of the fae; if you want to know more of the history, lore, and kinds of faeries, there are many excellent books out there on the topic, some of which I've included in Sources and Recommended Reading.

All that said, I believe in the fae and work with them on a . . . well, not daily basis . . . but seasonal basis. I tend to do magical workings involving the fae during the spring and summer months (their prime time is the Beltane and Midsummer sabbats), when the sun is reaching its peak and when nature is in full bloom around us. Admittedly, I do also work with faeries when I'm in need of a little extra oomph and inspiration for my writing, since I've been told many times by a variety of mystics that I have a number of fair folk on my spirit team who guide and inspire me in my work.

Faery Garden

When the lands of Faerie and the human world entwine, all is empowered and made more beautiful. The human world becomes more ensouled, and the missing pieces of our broken hearts are found again in the simplest and sometimes the most powerful of ways. For the faeries, I cannot speak, but it would seem to me that, if we have been able to do so much harm, we must be able to bring solutions, creative and compassionate, in their place.

—LUCY CAVENDISH

If you work closely with the fae, you might consider creating a faery garden.

There are some who believe creating a faery garden is inviting in fae of all kinds—the good, the mischievous, and those in between. But again, from my experience, the faeries I've encountered on my property, in my home, and in the nearby forest have been nothing but friendly. That's not to say there aren't mischief-making beings out there. My son swears up and down that there is a brownie in our house who hides his toys and games, although he does keep a less-than-tidy room. I've simply not encountered the mischief-makers, so can only speak from my experiences with the helpful ones. The place where I work with them most is in my outdoor garden space.

I mentioned that I have a small, separate faery garden/altar in the corner of my garden space. Let me tell you a bit more about how it came to be. I wasn't always someone who worked with the fae in my craft. In fact, I didn't even begin working with the fair folk in depth until a few years ago when my son and I went on a hike, and he saw a fairy. He described it as a small creature that darted between the trees. It didn't have wings, and it didn't look like the fairies he'd seen on television or in movies. There was no textbook definition or description of faerie that he'd ever been introduced to; it was an inner knowing. My son simply *knew* that what he saw was a fairy.

When we moved into our current house, he spotted another one on our property. A few weeks after we moved, I, too, saw one in the local state park where I like to hike in the early mornings. Like my son had seen those years ago, I saw something flicker from the corner of my eye and knew deep down it was the fair folk. Since then, I've set up a dedicated indoor altar and outdoor space for the fae to come and go as they like.

My indoor fairy altar sits in the middle of a windowsill in my office. My outdoor fairy garden houses a birdbath, its base carved like a tree trunk with a little fairy door and windows. I have a small fairy statue next to it that lights up at night, a bowl of honey for offering, and a foxglove plant (a plant sacred to the fae that has the ability to keep mischievous fae at bay) that looms over a moss-covered altar that has stones, leaves, and other items from the earth on it.

I know the fae are part of my creativity process, and oftentimes I turn to them when I'm in need of some inspiration. I typically do this by sitting in front of my indoor fairy altar, lighting a white or violet candle, then performing a card pull from one of my fairy tarot/oracle decks.

Tips for Working with Fae

◊ The fae don't respond well to low energy and negativity, so if you choose to honor them, be sure to do so from a place of positivity.

◊ Declutter. The fair folk don't like clutter or messes. In fact, some say brownies tend to hide items when homes are out of order. (This is what I tell my son, at least.)

◊ Leave an offering of sweet cream or honey. Make sure whatever you leave for them outside is something nontoxic to animals as well. The fair folk are protectors of land and of local animals, so don't want to see harm come to them.

◊ Keep an organic garden. Toxic chemicals and herbicides repel the fae, so use natural bug repellents and fertilizers.

◊ Pick up litter. Honor the fae by disposing of any litter that may have blown into your outdoor space. Take it a step further and pick up litter you find on a walk or hike in a nearby woods.

◊ Believe. It's so easy to dismiss the fair folk as beings of fiction, but if you wish to work with them, then you need to believe in them and in the powers of their magic.

How to Recognize the Fae

The fae are always present, but they don't often make themselves known to our world; however, because witches have a strong belief in other planes and are in touch with nature, fae are more likely to make their presence known to them. Many think they are invisible, but they sometimes choose to reveal themselves to certain people—particularly magical, mystical people. There are things you can look for that indicate faeries are nearby and possibly willing to work with you.

◊ Sweet scents. If you're working in your garden or going on a nature hike and get a sudden whiff of flowers and herbs but can't find any nearby, the fae may be close.

◊ A tickle on your cheek. It's thought that a tickle on your cheek (especially when there's no wind) indicates that the fae are near.

◊ Fairy ring of clover or mushrooms. Fairy rings have been spoken about for centuries and are places where faeries congregate. If you notice any rings of mushrooms, small flowers, or clover, the fae may be near.

◊ Flowers growing in unexpected places. A telltale sign of the fair folk is flowers growing in areas you'd least expect.

◊ Jewelry or stones gone missing. Some say faeries are attracted to items that shine and sparkle, so if you notice some of your jewelry or gemstones are missing, the fae may be to blame.

◊ You see spheres of light. Spheres and streaks of light seen from the corner of your eye could signal that a fairy is near.

◊ Animals around you begin to act strangely. Birds singing in unison or flying in unusual patterns indicates the presence of the fae.

◊ Laughter and high-pitched giggling when no children or other critters are around are a strong indication that the fae are nearby.

We faery folk are everywhere. We all play our part, and we have earned our place here at the table, with its feast of spirituality, as we are old, and the very bones upon which other faiths hang their clothes.

—LUCY CAVENDISH

1. *Rosemary. Rosemary is a common herb with both culinary and magical uses. In fact, many witches find rosemary a good substitute in magical workings for when other herbs can't be found. Rosemary can be used to repel bugs and has a fresh scent that's used in aromatherapy. It's one of the easiest herbs to grow, as it can withstand sun and heat. When it comes to magical workings, rosemary is useful in protection, love, and cleansing spells and rituals.*

2. *Lavender. Oh, lavender. With its unmistakable scent, lavender flowers are often used in pouches, sachets, and incense. It's also one of the most common essential oils and one of the few that can be placed directly on the skin. The plant aides in digestion and contains antiseptic properties. Its magic is associated with love, self-love, relaxation, protection, and purification.*

3. *Mugwort. Closely associated with wormwood, mugwort is known to enhance divination, psychic powers, and prophetic dreaming. Medicinally, it has a history of helping with menstruation, and can be used as an antiseptic and to tame tummy problems. Many witches use it in a simple infusion and drink it to induce clairvoyance. Mugwort is often added to incense blends during divination practices.*

4. *Sage. Sage is most popularly known for smudging—its dried leaves are burned, and the smoke is used for cleansing, warding off evil, and clearing spaces of negative energies. Medicinally, it has anti-inflammatory properties, may help with fever, and is a natural diuretic. Inhaling the scent of sage is thought to enhance memory and cognition.*

5. *Peppermint.* Historically, peppermint has been known to improve headaches, relieve congestion, and assist with circulation. Many people (myself included) like to sip on peppermint tea to help with digestive issues. Peppermint essential oil mixed with a carrier oil or lotion is great for sore and fatigued muscles and joints when applied topically. Magically, peppermint is used in money/abundance spells, healing spells, and rituals for purification.

6. *Other popular witch's herbs:* catnip, eucalyptus, lemon balm, rose

CHAPTER 6

Self-Care

By combining the elements of modern witchcraft with the mental health and wellness practice of self-care, you are creating a sacred space that honors all of your needs, not just those that are visible on the surface.

—TENAE STEWART

WITCHY SELF-CARE

What brings more comfort than a bit of self-care? In my book, nothing. I think of all the forms that self-care can take—reading a favorite book, sipping on tea, walking through the garden, a long ritual bath, watching *Good Witch* (okay, so that last one is a favorite self-care item of mine).

Taking time for ourselves de-stresses, and doing so with a touch of magic makes it that much better. When I think of magical self-care, my mind immediately goes to a long soak in the bath with a mug of tea, followed by a cuddling under a blanket with my dogs in my lap and either a good book in my hands or watching one of my favorite television shows or movies.

But there is so much more to self-care than pampering ourselves, especially when it comes to magical self-care. Self-care does, indeed, include pampering the physical body, but it's also about finding presence and mindfulness, creating a meditation routine, the act of relaxing, and working with plants and herbs (in conjunction with traditional medicine, if needed) to be our best selves.

It's also recognizing the need to rest and just *be* in times when we feel we *should* be doing. And as I've I said before, if we're not caring for ourselves, then how can we care for others?

MY REINTRODUCTION TO MEDITATION

About seven years ago, I went through one of the most difficult periods of my life. I was working full time as a high school English teacher when I had a panic attack in the middle of teaching a poetry lesson on figurative language. I could say the anxiety attack came unannounced, but it had been building over the prior few months.

Many nights, I'd had obsessive thoughts, my mind wandering to the worst possible outcome, many times irrational, of any situation. My thoughts were constantly screaming *what if?!* What if I fall down the stairs while home alone with my two-year-old? What if we get in a wreck on the way home from the grocery store? What if my son gets kidnapped from daycare? What if my husband slips on the ice and cracks his head open? What if . . . ? What if . . . ? What if . . . ? (Not comfy at all, right?)

At the time, I had no clue that I was dealing with a generalized anxiety disorder. I would push the thoughts aside, only for them to reappear at random times, usually the most inopportune ones (before doing a book talk to three hundred elementary school students comes to mind!). But the intrusive thoughts happened more and more frequently until that day in class when I was positive I was having a heart attack due to my rapid pulse, jittery hands, and uncontrollable mind spiral. And once I got that heart attack idea into my head, even more symptoms manifested, so much so that when I got home from work, I compulsively checked my blood pressure no less than one hundred times. Naturally, with the numbers rising every time due to the anxiety.

I used my essential oils, performed some calming rituals, did some mindful movement, but my anxiety continued to spiral beyond my control. I luckily got in to see my doctor that evening. My resting heart rate was over 130 beats per minute, I couldn't keep my feet from nervously tapping on the ground, and I shouted at the nurse to get away from me as she attempted to put the blood pressure cuff on my upper arm. (I literally tore the cuff from my arm.)

My doctor came in and knowing I was someone with a two decade–long thyroid condition, the first thing she did was order that my thyroid levels be checked. She performed an EKG to allay my heart attack fears and sent me home with melatonin and a prescription to help me get a good night's sleep before our appointment the next afternoon.

Well, needless to say, sleep didn't happen (that night and for many nights following). Instead, I paced from the kitchen to the dining room to the living room and back, while my body trembled uncontrollably (I couldn't even sip a cup of water without spilling it all over myself). My husband reminded me over and over that I wasn't dying. That I was dealing with anxiety. And that we would hopefully have some answers in the morning.

The next morning came, and before I could even make it in for my follow-up appointment, my doctor called. As it turned out, my thyroid stimulating hormone (TSH) levels came back barely detectible at an astonishingly low .02. I was being over medicated, having swung into severe hyperthyroidism, and was told to immediately cease taking my thyroid medication as it was toxic to my body. When I went in to see my doctor that afternoon, she explained that I would probably feel this way until the thyroid medicine left my body (it took six months for it to completely clear). She said that over time the anxiety would lessen. In the meantime, she gave me a prescription for a fast-acting medication for my panic attacks and set me up with an amazing therapist whom I saw three times a week.

Before that horrible episode, I had been meditating on and off for years, but it wasn't until I started therapy that I was introduced to the man whose mindfulness meditation techniques changed my life—Jon Kabat-Zinn. Now I could go on about Kabat-Zinn for a long time, but that's not the point of this chapter (or this book). Kabat-Zinn helped me to understand the concept that we are *human beings—not* human *doings.* He helped me to realize the need to be paying attention to our thoughts, in the present, nonjudgmentally. To not be swept away by *what ifs* and intrusive thoughts and not to get caught up in the anxiety spiral.

His ideas, coupled with some much-needed traditional medication, helped me get through the next two months of near-constant anxiety, and his grounding techniques are something that have enhanced my witchcraft practice in more ways than I could ever have imagined.

After all, as I said before, being mindful, in the present, and grounding yourself are the basis to any magical working. So when I'm in my head, when I'm not paying attention to my self-care, when I'm doing too much *doing* and not enough *being,* I suffer, which means my practice suffers right along with me.

So why am I telling you all this? Well, I feel that many people can relate to stories of suffering from anxiety. In fact, dozens of people have reached out regarding their own anxieties and how it hinders their practice. I'm also telling you to emphasize how much I *know* our thoughts and mental state controls, well, everything else. Sure, my anxiety was medically induced; however, after talking with my therapist and reflecting on many moments in my life, I realized that my general anxiety disorder had always been there, bubbling under the surface. And now that I've been to that horrible space, it's easier than ever to slip right back into it.

What does this have to do with being a witch? When we're not in a great headspace, our witchcraft won't be as powerful as when we're grounded and in a good energetic headspace. When I went through my period of severe anxiety, I was not doing much practicing of my craft. Honestly, I wasn't doing anything for myself other than worrying unnecessarily. So when I say mindfulness and grounding are the basis for my life and for all magical workings, I mean it. I know it's true because I've lived it.

Meditation

Throughout the last seven years, since I've really come back to my practice, meditation has played a big part. If you can't be completely grounded, it's much more difficult to do any work with energy because your thoughts are scattered, so the energy is scattered. There are many ways to ground yourself, but my favorite and most effective method is through meditation.

I meditate not only for my magical workings but also to help control my "monkey mind." Meditation is a tool to break away from those intrusive thoughts and quiet your mind enough to connect with higher spiritual powers and with your higher self. Your mind is in control of so much of your energy, so it's important to know how to control and ground that energy.

According to Jon Kabat-Zinn, meditating is the awareness that arises from paying attention, on purpose, in the present moment, and nonjudgmentally. Let's break that down a bit.

Awareness: the state of being aware or cognizant of something

Paying attention: paying attention to your breath, paying attention to the sounds around you, paying attention to your body and bodily sensations, paying attention to taste and other senses

On purpose: making it a point to pay attention

In the present moment: all about the sensations in the present; not thinking about "what ifs" that could happen in the future, not thinking about "should haves" that get us caught in the past, but being in the present—noticing things and sensations that ground us and keep us in the present moment

Nonjudgmentally: without any judgment whatsoever

When many people begin a meditation practice, they have a tendency to judge themselves. They're afraid that they're doing it wrong because they can't clear their mind, or because their mind keeps wandering. The main thing about a meditation practice is that it should be nonjudgmental. Your mind wanders. So what? If it wanders, then just come back to something in the present—a sound, your breath, a feeling in your body, counting on your fingers, something you're looking at. Coming back to that present moment is the important part, not judging yourself for getting off track.

Many people go into meditation thinking that they need to completely clear their mind. Meditation is actually not about clearing your mind—at all. It's about being aware of what's happening in your mind and what's happening in that present moment. In fact, you don't actually want to clear your mind. It's simply acknowledging things that come up and then going back to something that is occurring in the present—touch, breath, movements, and more.

Meditation and Witchcraft

Our craft and practice is all about working with energy and manipulating energy to make a change. (To make some magic!) When we are grounded, when we are mindful, because we're in a relaxed state of awareness, we're able to sense energies even better and able to work with our magic in a more effective way.

Meditation grounds us. Grounding helps us connect with our higher self, connect with ancestors, connect with spirit, connect with deity, and prepare our bodies for ritual. It also quiets our mind enough to hear messages from guides, ancestors, spirit. The mere act of meditation also opens up our "clair" senses—claircognizance, clairvoyance, clairaudience, clairsentience, clairalience, and clairgustance. It allows for better astral travel and path work.

That said, before I do any sort of magical working, even if it's something as small as creating a small spell bottle, I make sure I'm grounded first.

Meditation Misconceptions

I want to debunk some of the misconceptions regarding meditating. As mentioned earlier, many people believe that meditating means completely clearing your mind. This is not the case at all. The point of meditation is to connect yourself to the present. To hear a thought, acknowledge it, and then move on from it.

I've always liked the "boiling pot" analogy. When it comes to your thoughts while meditating, observe them like a bubble boiling to the surface. Watch the thought bubble float to the surface. It pops. Then you move on to the next item without attaching yourself to it or letting it capture you. This allows you to remain present, simply an observer of thoughts.

The next misconception about meditating is that you have to focus on your breath. Personally, I struggle to focus on my breath. I often find myself asking, "Am I breathing too fast, too slow, enough?" And I've been meditating for years! I'm pretty sure this goes along with my health anxieties. It's something I'm still working on, but know that there are many, many other ways to be mindful without the breathwork—mindful movement, tactile meditation, visual meditation.

Another misconception is that only experienced meditators can meditate. Absolutely not. Anyone can meditate. In fact, my seven-year-old son meditates with me. He practices mindfulness with what he calls his "sunshine breath" by raising his hands over his head and then bringing them down, over and over again. When his arms go up, he envisions the sun going up. When his arms come down, he envisions the sun going down. He also does a snake breath where he inhales deeply, and on the exhale, he hisses and moves his body back and forth like a snake. It's equal parts adorable and magical to watch him do this.

As soon as you sit down to meditate, you're meditating.

Meditation Methods

Below are some ways to meditate. If you're just starting out, I recommend setting a timer for five to ten minutes and practicing one or more of the exercises below. The most important thing to remember is this: *if you have an intrusive thought while meditating—that is okay!* Simply acknowledge it, then move back to whatever it is you're focusing on in that present moment.

Breath. The most common method of meditating is focusing on your breath (not my preferred method, however). Close your eyes, take a few deep breaths, then settle into your normal breathing pattern. Focus on your breath and the sensations that come along with each inhale and exhale. In through your nose, out through your mouth. If a thought pops into your mind, acknowledge it, but then come right back to your breath. Take it a magical step further. With every breath you take in, imagine you're inhaling calm and joy and radiance. With every exhale, imagine you're letting go of all of those worries and things that have been bothering you.

Counting. Simply counting can be a mindful meditation. Not counting your breaths (which you may choose to do) but just counting; close your eyes and count slowly to ten, over and over. If your mind wanders to other thoughts while you're counting, that's okay. Just acknowledge the thought and go back to counting. If you prefer to count to a different number, say forty-seven (my personal favorite), then do that. The most important thing is that you're focusing on the counting and not latching on to any thoughts or other sensations during your counting meditation.

Sounds. Simply listening and paying attention, on purpose, to sounds in the present moment is meditating. See if you can tune in to the sounds around you while you sit to meditate. If you're outside, focus on the birds chirping in a nearby tree. Maybe you'll notice the passing of cars and traffic. Perhaps you're inside on a rainy day. Focus on the sound of the raindrops dripping off your roof and onto the sidewalk or ground below. Again, if any other thoughts arise, acknowledge them, then come back to the sounds in the present moment.

Movement. One of my favorite ways to meditate is through movement. You do not have to be sitting still on a meditation cushion listening to your breath to be meditating. Get the preconceived notion of having to stay still out of your head. There is much to be said about mindful moving meditation. There are walking meditations in which you can focus on the ground beneath your feet and the sensations and feelings throughout your body as you move. Another type of walking meditation is to focus on counting your steps. I often do this when I'm doing a mindful meditative walk around the block.

Touch. If you're a tactile person, you can meditate using the sensations of touch. With each inhale of air, run a finger up your forearm; with each exhale, run it back down. Pay attention to that sensation on your arm the entire time. Start with five minutes, work up to ten, then twenty, and beyond. And if your mind wanders . . . that's fine. Come back to the sensation on your arm and keep going.

Visualization. Visual work is another great way to meditate, and a way that is preferred by many witches. In meditating this way you simply envision a white light coming down from the sky and moving slowly through your body from the feet up. Notice the sensations that you feel as the light scans down your body. You can take this a step further and envision the light cleansing each body part as it moves. If you have aphantasia, like me, this may not be your preferred style of meditating.

Body scan. Another popular form of mindful meditation is done by performing a body check-in scan. Like the light visualization, start at your feet and work your way up to the crown of your head, feeling the sensations in each body part as you go along. If you get to a body part that feels uneasy or tense, acknowledge that feeling, relax that muscle, then move on to the next body part. As usual, if your mind wanders, come back to being in your body.

Guided. If you need a bit of extra guidance, there are many guided meditations available in books and on phone apps. My favorite app for guided meditations is Insight Timer. It's free and has thousands of guided meditations on any mundane or magical topic you can think of: reducing anxiety, being happier, connecting with the moon cycle, connecting with your inner witch, and so much more.

While performing any of these meditations, pay attention to any messages you may receive from your guides. When our mind is quiet, it's easier for our spirit teams to convey messages to us, whether through words, visuals, sounds, smells, or even tastes. Take a mental note of any message you get and jot it down once you've completed your meditation. I've had some of the most amazing messages come through during a simple everyday meditation.

Starting Small

Put on some of your favorite music (no words)—my favorite thing to do is tell Alexa to "play meditation music." Light your favorite incense or candle. Surround yourself with your favorite crystals. Close your eyes and try one of the techniques above. Count your breath. Count your steps. Scan your body. Whatever you choose to do, know that by simply trying it, you're doing it right!

GROUNDING

So I've used the word *"grounding"* many times throughout this book and thought it time to define the term a bit. When you ground yourself, you're drawing energy from the earth to stabilize yourself and bring you back into a positive state in the present moment.

Grounding makes you aware of your body and the energy and magic coursing through it. It is our direct connection to the magic that runs through Mother Earth—the energy and magic coursing through her since the beginning of time. Imagine being able to connect with that ancient energy and the opportunities that can arise by doing so.

You already know my favorite way to ground and center myself, but I've listed a few more below. Grounding makes me instantly feel comfy, cozy, and connected to my practice.

Nature. *Get out in nature.* Take a stroll through your backyard or, if you live in an urban area, go outside and take a walk around town or in a local park. It's even better if you can connect directly to that earth. Walk barefoot outside and feel the earth's energy and magic move up your legs, through your body, filling your entire being.

Water. Another great way to ground yourself is to connect with the element of water. Get in or near running water of some kind. Place your hands in a local spring or even just turn on the faucet and let the water run over your fingers. Water is a great conductor of energy, and merely touching it connects you to earth's natural springs. I particularly enjoy listening to the trickling water in my garden fountain. Between that and being in my garden, I feel the most connected to nature and my root here more than anywhere else.

Animals. I'm sure you've heard of the studies conducted that claim simply petting an animal every day increases happiness and may even contribute to a longer life. I would have to agree. Our domestic pets calm, comfort, and ground us with one simple touch, and observing animals in nature has the same effect. Simply touch or get near an animal to connect with the grounding energy of earth's many creatures. Personally, I find it the most grounding when I'm petting one of my dogs or watching the birds and deer (and sometimes a fox friend) prance around my backyard.

Crystals. Stones have been around since the beginning of time—I mean, the earth is made of layers of rock. Because of this, the simple act of touching or being near one has an immediate grounding effect and connects you to earth's innate magic. Although there are hundreds of gemstones and crystals that can be used for grounding, some of my personal favorites are tiger's eye, clear quartz, smoky quartz, red jasper, black obsidian, and bloodstone. When you're looking for some comfort or need to take a moment to check in with yourself, hold your favorite stone in your hand, rub your thumb over its smooth surface, and take a few deep breaths.

Visualizations. If you don't have the ability to get outside, pet an animal, or grab a crystal, it's possible to ground yourself anywhere through the act of visualization. You can do this by taking a comfortable seat on the ground. Close your eyes and inhale deeply three times. Next, imagine your root chakra area (right where your bum meets the ground) glowing a vibrant red. Imagine that red turns into roots that reach and stretch into the ground with each inhale, connecting you directly to the earth. (If you struggle to envision within your mind's eye, like me, simply narrate aloud what you should be imagining.)

SCENTS

Another thing that grounds me and helps clear my mind is scent. One of the fastest ways to raise energy, ground yourself, or prepare for a magical working is smelling specific scents. Certain aromas relax, heal, energize, promote creativity and productivity, increase romance, cleanse negativity, call in helpful spirits . . . truly, the list goes on and on.

Any time someone new comes to our home and they're given a small tour, they always comment on how great my office smells. And they are not wrong. Yes, I live with two boys and two dogs—and my son is at an age where showering is decidedly not his favorite thing to do—so I am well aware that not every room in our house smells particularly sweet. However, my indoor sacred space always, and I mean *always*, smells divine. Honestly, I can't pinpoint the scent in my office, as it's an amalgamation of dozens of various herbs, oils, incenses, and candles; what I can pinpoint is the feeling of calm that immediately overtakes me (and others) when I step into this space and take a deep breath.

One of my favorite parts of my morning ritual is lighting herbs, incense, or a scented candle. I get such satisfaction from doing this. I typically choose my scents depending on the season. As I write this, it's summer, and I'm in my office, which you now know doubles as my sacred space. Today, a lavender and eucalyptus candle burns not two feet in front of me. The lavender is sweet and calming, while the eucalyptus adds a touch of vibrance and clarity, both things I need while getting to work.

When I'm in this space in the early mornings, I light my black and white candles and use the candle flames to light my incense for that particular meditation session. This morning, I went with frankincense incense, which I've been burning a lot lately. The lotion I applied just a few minutes ago is scented with lemongrass and rosemary. It's no wonder my office smells so heavenly. These magical scents are with me every part of the day, a constant comfort, and because I use the scents for specific intentions, when I catch a whiff of them, they bring me right back to my practice and their intended uses.

A Very Brief History of Aromatherapy

Aromatherapy has been around for thousands of years, and even the ancients knew the effect that scents could have on minds and bodies.

Early Egyptians used oils in the creation of salves and tinctures that they created for healing and spiritual rights. Cleopatra had spa treatments consisting of salt from the Dead Sea mixed with essential oils (many of the clay and salt treatments were thought to have been gifted to her by Mark Antony).

The Greek physician Hippocrates, once considered the father of medicine, studied and recorded the medicinal uses of over two hundred plants. From his studies, he noted the benefit of aromatherapy in ritual baths and massage.

Literature from 2000 BC boasts the use of oils in the Indian Ayurvedic health system, which blends spiritual, philosophical, and physical elements. In fact, the Vedas, India's sacred prayers and religious texts, mentions the use of over seven hundred herbs and oils for healing.

In Rome, oils were used to scent the hair, body, and bedsheets of everyone from nobles to peasants.

The oldest surviving Chinese medical text (2700 BC) contained information on over 365 plants and their uses. And China's mythical ruler Shennong, credited as the father of Chinese herbal medicine, is said to have tested hundreds of herbs for their medicinal value.

We even see references to aromatherapy and use of oils throughout the Christian Bible.

Scent Methods

There are many methods to diffuse a scent in your home. The mere action of diffusing an oil, or lighting a candle, or burning herbs not only makes you house smell wonderful, but when done with purpose and intention, it's also a way to connect to spirit, open communication with deity, raise energy in a space, and clear away any energies or emotions that don't serve you. Not only that, but scents also remind us of our connection to earth and its elemental and healing properties more than other senses. Just think of the power and magic in smell, how one sniff of a familiar aroma can transport us to the past, reigniting treasured feelings and memories we had thought long forgotten.

Scents can be diffused into your home in a plethora of ways, most of which I've listed below.

Incense. Burning incense for worship, meditation, and prayer is thought to have been done as early as 3300 BC. Made from a combination of plant materials and essential oils, incense is used today in therapy, meditation, prayer, and magical workings. Whether you like incense sticks, cones, or pellets, using it is a great way to connect with the divine. And it makes your home smell good, too. Its magical uses include clearing and cleansing, connecting with deity, and offerings.

Herb burning. The idea of burning herbs in a bundled form to transform, clear, or enhance energy in a space has been done for thousands of years. In herb bundles, dried herbs are bound together with a cotton material, then burned; the smoke serves to cleanse and purify a space. Another method of herb burning is to light a charcoal disk in a fire-proof vessel and then sprinkle pinches of dried herbs on top. *Note: Be cautious when burning oils, herbs, and incense around animals and small children.*

Oils. The first records of essential oil extracts come from ancient India, Egypt, and Rome where oils were used in consecration rituals, prayer, and as offerings to deity. Ancient Egyptians were thought to use aromatic oils in their makeup products as early as 4500 BC. These oils are formed by concentrating essences from different parts of plants. You can diffuse oils in an oil burner or an aromatherapy mister. I like to diffuse oils for aromatherapy by putting a few drops of oil into a mug of boiling water. Various scents and combinations work together in healing and magical workings.

Mists. Aromatherapy sprays and mists are a combination of essential oils, flowers, and gemstones in pure water; use the power of intention to cleanse a space, to work with emotions, and to change the energy of a space. You'll find my recipe for a lovely magical misting spray at the end of the chapter.

Candles. A popular way to infuse scent into a space is by burning candles. For my magical workings, I use beeswax candles that burn quickly; but for aromatherapy and everyday burning, I prefer candles made from soy or vegetable wax. I also look for candles made with pure essential oils rather than chemical-based fragrances. Like incense, candles can assist you with manifestation and intention-setting when you light them with a specific purpose in mind.

Magical Scents

Below are some of my favorite scents that I use on a regular basis; they immediately make me feel calm and grounded. Because these are some of my absolute favorites, you'll noticed the corresponding herbs and essential oils used in a number of the recipes throughout the book.

This list is not exhaustive, but I've included many of the most commonly used herbs for healing and magic. The great thing about these are how easily accessible they are, and many can be foraged in the wild or grown in your own witch's garden.

Cedar—cedar is innately earthy and draws upon both earth and divine energies, making it both grounding and spiritual at the same time. It has the ability to calm, and it strengthens health and clarity for working with spirit.

Magical uses: cleansing, clarity, protection, encourages meditation

Cinnamon—I work with cinnamon on a daily basis, adding it to my morning cup of coffee and calling in the intentions of warmth and grounding. Cinnamon is known to aid in digestion, circulation, and inflammation. Using cinnamon oil with clove is thought to assist in regulating blood sugar. It has a high vibration, brings much warmth and joy, and gets your energy moving in a healthy way.

Magical uses: warmth, healing, passion, joy, spirituality

Eucalyptus—I love hanging fresh eucalyptus from my shower head, allowing the steam to release its fresh scent. Eucalyptus is known for its cooling and healing properties.

Magical uses: healing, happiness, purification, energizing

Frankincense—frankincense is one of my go-to fragrances. It's thought to assist good digestion and enhance the immune system. I look to frankincense when I am working with spirit in any way—meditating, connecting with the divine, working in my sacred space.

Magical uses: lifting vibrations, meditation work, deity work

Lavender—lavender is arguably the most popular scent used in aromatherapy. The benefits of this magical herb have been known for thousands of years. Not only does the scent evoke an immediate sense of calm, but lavender is also known to be an antioxidant, antimicrobial, sedative, tranquilizer, and antidepressant. I grab lavender when I'm in need of relaxation and frequently add it to my body products—scrubs, bath salts, and oils.

Magical uses: peace, longevity, happiness, protection, love

Lemon balm—one of my favorite scents, lemon balm is summer in an herb, reducing stress, anxiety, nervousness, and assisting with sleep and relaxation. For an ultimate restful sleep, combine lemon balm and lavender essential oils.

Magical uses: healing, love, friendship, prosperity, abundance

Peppermint—a hybrid of water mint and spearmint, peppermint is known for its refreshing taste and scent. Although many associate it with the winter season, I use peppermint on those sweltering summer days when my skin is in need of some cooling. Peppermint is known to ease stomach issues and headaches and to be a reliever of cold and fever.

Magical uses: healing, focus, purification, travel, psychic powers

Rose—rose is commonly associated with love and many self-care rituals, but it's also known to ease bladder infections and inflammations and boost heart health. I often add dried rose petals to my bath salts for ritual baths. Rose is also known to raise vibrations to a very high level of pure sweetness and love.

Magical uses: healing, love, luck, friendship, calming emotions, heart-opening

Rosemary—another one of my favorites, rosemary has been used in witchcraft for centuries and is used by many witches as a substitute herb when they're lacking a specific one. Rosemary is connected to the memory, recall, and cognition. It's known to improve mood and ease anxiety.

Magical uses: healing, sleep, cognitive abilities, purification

Sage—with its Latin name *salvia* meaning "to save," sage is one of the most popular herbs used by witches. It's known to cleanse the air and assist with memory issues, as well as help infections, sore muscles, tension, and sore throats.

Magical uses: cleansing, wisdom, immortality, longevity

Valerian—found by ancient Greeks to be the go-to herb for calming anxiety, valerian is another herb known for assisting in sleep; valerian can calm the nervous system and help quell anxiety and stress. It's also a great herb to use when trying to release feelings of guilt and when looking for acceptance.

Magical uses: sleep, deep relaxation, ending guilt, forgiveness

BATH MAGIC

After a long, exhausting day (especially in winter), what I most look forward to is a long soak in a hot bathtub. Water, being one of the four elements, is connected to our emotions, the ebbs and flows of life, purification, protection, and rebirth. It makes sense, then, that so many of us turn to the bath or shower in our magical self-care practices for healing, rejuvenation, and relaxation. And when we charge our bath water with intention and the addition of salts, oils, herbs, and crystals, it's that much more powerful.

Taking a thirty-minute (or longer) salt bath at the beginning of each week is a great way to cleanse yourself and release toxins and toxic energy through your pores, getting you prepared for the week. What I love most about salt baths is that you don't need many ingredients, and you can oftentimes create the bath salts in less than two minutes (recipe at the end of the chapter).

MAGICAL SELF-CARE

We've chatted in this chapter about self-care in the form of grounding, meditation, and aromatherapy, and in the previous chapters I've detailed self-care in the forms of gardening, cooking, holding sacred space, reading, and more. Here I give a quick run-down of activities that you can do to take a moment away from the hustle and bustle of life to focus on yourself.

They might seem obvious and simple enough, but too few witches actually take a moment to do them. Performing simple self-care rituals tells us that we honor ourselves and our bodies, automatically making us feel more grounded and connected to our practices.

So here's my challenge to you . . . every day for the next week, choose an item (or two) from the list below to mindfully and intentionally complete. Schedule it into your planner if need be. Put a sign on the bedroom door that reads "ME TIME" so anyone else in the house knows not to disturb you. Making time for yourself through intentional self-care is inherently magical and lends itself to even better spell and ritual work. After all, a clear mind and relaxed spirit are essential to performing your best household magic.

◊ Read a book of your choosing for at least twenty minutes

◊ Grab a cozy blanket and cuddle with a pet

◊ Draw yourself a hot bath

◊ Make a cup of tea and drink it slowly

◊ Take a nap and don't feel guilty about it

◊ Journal your frustrations in a notebook

◊ Meditate for fifteen minutes

◊ Create a playlist of songs that make you feel magical and listen to them

◊ Take a twenty-minute walk outside

◊ Light a candle, incense, or diffuse an oil and enjoy the scent

◊ Buy yourself a fresh bouquet of flowers

◊ Give yourself a facial or manicure

◊ Craft: color, knit, or create something that excites you

SELF-CARE RECIPES AND RITUALS

Here are the promised recipes. Use them and enjoy them. Your practice can only benefit from taking some "me time."

※ ¡ ※

Bath Salts Recipe

Add these salts to your bath for a relaxing, rejuvenating, and uplifting experience. Here is a recipe for your basic bath salts; however, choose specific oils, herbs, and crystals according to your intention.

You'll need:

> 1 cup sea salt
>
> ½ cup Epsom salts
>
> 12 drops essential oil
>
> 1 teaspoon dried herbs
>
> (see oil and herb blends to align with intentions below)

Mix all ingredients together. Light a candle or incense, turn on some relaxing music, sprinkle the salt mixture in your bathwater, and enjoy!

SUGGESTED OIL AND HERB BATH BLENDS BY INTENTION

◊ **Anxiety:** combine twelve drops lavender and one teaspoon dried lemon balm

◊ **Depression:** combine six drops lemon oil, six drops grapefruit oil, one teaspoon thyme

◊ **Guilt:** combine six drops pine oil, six drops eucalyptus oil, one teaspoon mint

◊ **Worry:** combine six drops sage oil, six drops lavender oil, one teaspoon dried chamomile

◊ **Overcoming obstacles:** combine six drops basil oil, six drops frankincense, one teaspoon mint

◊ **Sleep:** combine six drops lavender oil, six drops chamomile oil, one teaspoon rosemary

◊ **Love:** combine six drops rose oil, six drops lavender oil, handful rose petals

◊ **Warmth and protection:** combine six drops cinnamon oil, three drops orange oil, three drops clove oil, one teaspoon dried chamomile

Room Mist Recipe

Instead of buying a room spray or mist, you can create your own using this simple recipe. Use corresponding oils, herbs, and gemstones to charge your sprays with a specific intention.

You'll need:

1 cup water

1 teaspoon witch hazel

26 drops essential oil

pinch of herbs, flower petals, or spices

2–3 crystal chips

(see oil and herb blends aligned with intentions below)

In a bowl, mix together the water, witch hazel, and essential oils. Pour the mixture into two four-ounce spray bottles. Add the herbs, flower petals, spices, and crystal chips. Put the spray nozzle on top and use in whatever space you choose.

SUGGESTED OIL, HERB, AND CRYSTAL BLENDS FOR ROOM MISTS

◊ **Anxiety blend:** combine thirteen drops lavender oil, seven drops lemon balm oil, and six drops rosemary oil. Add a lavender sprig and peridot chips.

◊ **Cleansing blend** (my favorite blend for my sacred spaces): combine eighteen drops lavender oil and eight drops sage oil. Add dried sage leaves and citrine chips.

◊ **Love/self-love blend:** combine thirteen drops rose oil and thirteen drops lavender oil. Add rose petals and rose quartz crystal chips.

◊ **Warmth and protection blend:** combine thirteen drops orange oil, seven drops cinnamon oil, and six drops clove oil. Add two cloves and tiger's eye chips.

◊ **Meditation blend:** combine thirteen drops frankincense oil, thirteen drops lemon oil. Add a piece of orange peel and crystal quartz chips.

❧ ⚲ ❧

Healing Balm Recipe

Use this balm to aid in sleep or to help with congestion and allergy/cold symptoms.

You'll need:

5 tablespoons shea butter

1 tablespoon coconut oil

2 drops rosemary oil

2 drops peppermint oil

2 drops lavender oil

2 drops pine oil

2 drops eucalyptus oil

Melt the shea butter in a double boiler. If you don't have that capability, heat the butter in thirty-second increments in the microwave until melted. Remove from heat and stir in the coconut oil. Quickly add the essential oils drops and mix thoroughly. Pour the mixture into a tin and let the balm solidify and cool. Cover with a lid. To use, apply topically under your nose, on your chest, or on the bottoms of your feet.

Note: You can use any combination of essential oils for specific intentions. For example, use rose and lavender oils for a love/self-love balm; peppermint and eucalyptus for a stress-reduction balm; or cinnamon, clove, and orange oils for a protection balm.

Salt Bath Ritual

Much like the healing baths of ancient Rome, a ritual bath is meant to cleanse your aura, rebalance your energy centers, and leave you feeling recharged and abundant in self-care and love.

You'll need:

pre-made magical bath salts (from recipe above)

candles for ambiance and to enhance intention (optional)

Fill your bathtub with water to the temperature of your liking. Once filled, get in the bath and hold the ritual salts in your hand. Say, *"May these salts protect, cleanse, and revitalize me."*

Pour the salts into the water and stir them deosil (clockwise) while repeating the words above three times.

Enjoy the soothing scent of your bath and indulge in the self-care ritual. Clear your mind of the goings-on of the day and bask in the feel of the water and scent of the salts.

CHAPTER 7

Everyday Rituals

Any ritual is an opportunity for transformation.

—STARHAWK

Finding Magic in the Everyday Things

People (read witches) oftentimes beat themselves up if they aren't "witchy" enough. We have social media to thank for that; nevertheless, there is a push to be more magical, more witchy, and to document it all on Instagram or TikTok or the newest sharing platform. But I'm here to tell you as we get into this final chapter, none of that is necessary, nor does your social media presence define you or your craft. If you're able to check in to your practice once a day, then that is enough. And if you can check in only once a week, that's perfectly fine, too. Don't beat yourself up with negative self-talk and unattainable witchy goals.

As you know by now, I'm a huge advocate for finding magic in the everyday things, no matter how big or small. I'm constantly on the go—running my son to school events, keeping up with writing projects and deadlines, cooking, and maintaining a household. Because of this, on many days my formal practice is placed on the back burner. Sometimes we plan a beautiful day of connecting to our craft, but real life has other plans.

For example, I'm writing this on the heels of Lughnasadh, but I woke up a few days ago—on Lughnasadh morning, in fact—with a terrible migraine headache. I'd had great plans for some kitchen witchery—braided zucchini bread and fish on the grill—and even bigger plans for an evening ritual to honor the first of the harvest seasons. Alas, the migraine had me on the couch all day long. At first I was bummed; however, I knew if I had chosen to go ahead with baking the bread and doing a ritual, my heart and magic wouldn't have been in it. So I made my bread and performed my Lammas ritual three days later . . . no problem.

Just this morning I woke up to my son spilling an entire cereal bowlful of milk and Cheerios on the floor (I am grateful that he's independent enough to *attempt* making it on his own), so I spent what would usually be my morning ritual time helping him clean that up and then mopping the floor. Of course, that then turned into a deep cleaning of the kitchen because I noticed remnants of last night's spaghetti sauce on the stovetop. Needless to say, my morning ritual didn't happen as I'd intended it to. However, I still found ways to connect to my practice in small, meaningful ways throughout the day.

This chapter will focus on everyday rituals—big and small, formal and not—that keep us connected to our practice, no matter what the mundane throws our way.

Creating a Morning Ritual

A great way to connect to your practice and begin your day with magical intention is with a consistent morning ritual. I'm not talking about an everyday *routine*: wake up, shower, brush teeth, make breakfast, etc. A routine is something that, while you do it every day, you also do so on autopilot. Whereas a morning ritual is something you do on a daily basis with an inner knowing and with intention. While a routine allows monotony and a simple *going through the motions*, ritual is done with purpose and attention—and when it comes to a witch's ritual, it also includes magic in some way, shape, or form.

Of all the topics I've covered on the Comfy Cozy Witch podcast, people comment most about the episode on setting up rituals, and many have told me they now do a morning ritual similar to mine and that it has made a big difference in their practice. I want to share my morning ritual with you. Feel free to borrow any part of it to incorporate into your own daily ritual.

I try to wake up most mornings before the rest of the household is awake so that I can have peace and quiet to myself. I love the very early morning, just before the sun rises, when the house is tranquil, and I can hear every creak of the floorboard and spit of the candle. To me, this is comfy coziness at its finest and when I can best touch base with my craft.

First, I make myself a cup of coffee (decaf because I don't tolerate caffeine well). I add a touch of cream and honey or maple syrup, then sprinkle a pinch of cinnamon on the top. I add cinnamon each morning for warmth. When I add the honey, I say, "I invite kindness to me," while stirring clockwise three times. When I add the cinnamon, I say, "I invite warmth and protection into my day," again stirring clockwise three times. I thank Goddess for another day, then take my coffee into my indoor sacred space. (Outdoor when weather permits, then continue with the rest of the ritual inside once I'm finished outside.)

Next, I have a seat either in front of my main altar or on the small carpet in front of the windowsill in my sacred space. It all depends on how I'm feeling and if my body would welcome the ground or my cushiony stool. At the time of writing this, I've been favoring the floor.

I light two candles—a black one for protection and to banish any negative energy, and a white one to welcome calm and light for the day. While I light the candles, I think about those two intentions.

Next, I do some light stretching, lifting my hands over my head, breathing deeply with each inhale. On the exhale, I let my arms fall to my sides. I repeat this three times, and it's on the third inhale when I invite my guides to join me for the day. I simply say, "I ask you, guides of my highest good, to join me for my day." I then proceed to do a bit of self-Reiki, typically lasting anywhere from two to ten minutes. (I'm a Usui Reiki master and became one just so I could perform Reiki on myself.)

Once I'm satisfied with the energy flow, I close my eyes for at least five minutes of meditation. I often meditate while listening to a playlist of orchestral music or I meditate to a guided meditation through the Insight Timer app.

After that, I pull out my book of shadows and begin journaling. I start each daily entry with the moon phase. Next, I list at least two things I'm grateful for. Keeping a daily gratitude list helps me focus on what magic is working in my life, and it forces me to be in the present moment. I then consult one or more of my oracle card or tarot decks for some daily guidance and then write out my intuitive thoughts about the card(s) pulled. This is when I also reflect on yesterday's card pull or card pulls from the few days prior to see if there's a theme or something my spirit team is trying to show me that I'm not yet seeing. This journaling process can take a minute or, as I've done in the past, it could take an hour or more.

I finish the morning ritual by thanking my guides, then blowing out the candles.

Making Time

My morning ritual can take anywhere from fifteen minutes to an hour or longer, depending on how much time I spend meditating and journaling and depending on how much time I have before I need to attend to the *mundane* parts of the day—making breakfast, getting my son off to school, getting in my daily word count, responding to emails, etc.

Many people have asked my advice on starting a routine, saying they simply don't have the time because their mornings are busy with kids' schedules, cooking, early work days, and the like. My response is to try your best to find the time. Do you often hit the snooze button over and over again? Set the alarm twenty minutes earlier than you usually wake up to ensure a quiet house and quiet sacred space to yourself. *It isn't the length of a ritual that matters, it's the quality. Touching your practice in one way, shape, or form for any amount of time will make a difference.*

On the other hand, I want to reiterate something: it is okay if you miss a day or two or a week or even more of your ritual. Life gets busy. Things come up. Vacations are needed. It's important not to stress over missing your daily ritual because the last thing you want to do is force yourself into your spiritual practice. That will make something so magical and sacred seem like a chore, which is the opposite of what you want to accomplish. However, I do know that even if I'm exhausted and the last thing I want to do is spend time meditating or pulling cards, as soon as I get into my sacred space and light those candles, I immediately feel calm and connected to my practice, which reminds me how magical this sacred time to myself is.

> *"It isn't the length of a ritual that matters, it's the quality."*

CREATING A NIGHTLY RITUAL

Just as I begin my day with a morning ritual, I end my day with an evening one. Although not as extensive as my morning ritual, my nighttime ritual is just as sacred to me. In fact, I haven't missed an evening ritual for over seven years.

After putting my son to bed, I spend some time either reading on the sofa or relaxing by catching up on some of my favorite television shows (hello, *Good Witch*). Once I'm ready for bed, I begin my evening ritual.

First, I do the mundane things—put on my pajamas and brush my teeth. Then I move on to my more magical items. I grab my favorite essential oil—lavender—and place a drop on the bottom of each foot and then a few more drops in my hand. Next I add a pump or two of unscented lotion (I like CeraVe) and mix the oil and lotion together in my hands. I rub this mixture across shoulders, neck, and arms, thanking my guides for being with me for my day. While I'm rubbing it in, I envision (speak aloud to myself) a cool lavender light encapsulating me, sending calming rays for a peaceful night's sleep.

I inhale three times, raising my arms up in a stretch with each inhale (similar to what I do during the morning ritual), and breathe in the lavender, inviting in calm and peace. When I lie down in bed, I pop in my earbuds and listen to a guided meditation from my favorite meditation app.

From an outsider's perspective, my nightly ritual might look like a routine—oil, lotion, music. But to me, it's a magical ritual for a peaceful slumber and intentional time spent focusing on that and communicating with my guides.

CONNECTING WITH THE ELEMENTS

Nature provides a vast collage of plants, flowers, herbs, food, precipitation, and other materials to work with, but I think we have a tendency to take these wonders for granted, forgetting that they're provided by the magic of Goddess and connected to the elemental energies of the universe.

Everything we encounter possesses qualities that correspond with one or more (or all) of the four elements. A simple way to be reminded of the magic all around us on a daily basis is by recognizing that those everyday things—the water we wash our face with, the fire lighting our hearth, the wind kissing our cheeks, the earth under our feet—are *components* of our spiritual practice not just mundane thoughts and actions.

Although we often use the elements in our practices through ritual work and at our altars, we often neglect to notice them outside that space and in the everyday. I challenge you to take notice and to connect with the elemental magic outside your workings and in the everyday. Below you'll find the four elements, correspondences, and everyday ways you can connect to them to stay in touch with your practice in a meaningful, albeit small, way.

Magic is all around us—if only we would look.

Earth Correspondences

Direction: north

Season: winter

Color: green, brown, black

Tarot: pentacles, pages

Astrological signs: Taurus, Virgo, Capricorn

Animals: bear, dog, deer, fox

Stones: emerald, peridot, tiger's eye, onyx

Herbs: cedar, sage, patchouli, vetiver, salt

Rules: physical body, nature, animals, death, money

Ways to connect: get out in nature, touch or be near running water, grow plants, connect with crystal energies, observe animals, play in the dirt, walk barefoot, practice mindfulness and meditation, step away from technology

Air Correspondences

Direction: east

Season: spring

Tarot: swords

Astrological signs: Aquarius, Gemini, Libra

Animals: eagle, raven, spider

Stones: citrine, topaz, sapphire, amethyst

Herbs: lavender, rosemary, lemongrass, cilantro

Rules: communication, thought

Ways to connect: light incense, clean your home, breathe deeply, speak charms and incantations, journal, collect feathers, plant fragrant herbs and flowers, smell the air after a storm

Fire Correspondences

Direction: south

Season: summer

Color: red, orange, gold, crimson

Tarot: wands

Astrological signs: Aries, Leo, Sagittarius

Animals: dragon, lion, horse, fox, snake

Stones: ruby, red jasper, fire opal, garnet, bloodstone

Herbs: cinnamon, garlic, pepper, hibiscus

Rules: creativity, passion, courage, healing, blood

Ways to connect: light a candle, perform candle magic, host a bonfire, move your body, gaze at the stars, soak up the sun's energy, sip on a hot beverage

Water Correspondences

Direction: west

Season: fall

Color: blue, turquoise, green, gray

Tarot: cups

Astrological signs: Cancer, Scorpio, Pisces

Animals: dolphin, fish, sea mammals, cats

Stones: aquamarine, amethyst, pearl, coral, lapis lazuli

Herbs: fern, willow, lotus, gardenia

Rules: emotions, intuition, cleansing, fertility

Ways to connect: go swimming, take a bath or shower, consecrate your magical tools, stay hydrated, practice self-care rituals, do something for you (read, nap, relax), use essential oils, journal about your emotions

Magic with Children

My son is full of wonder and a believer in magic of all kinds. The way he views magic in nature and the everyday is a sight to behold. Oftentimes, it's at my son's prompting that we go for a hike, set up offerings for the fae, or pull cards from our oracle card decks. And, yes, my son has two decks that he loves very much—an animal deck and a dragon deck—that he pulls from every morning.

He loves searching the woods for his faery friends, collecting rocks and assigning them magical powers, celebrating the sabbats and nature festivals, performing his own magic with his many wands and Harry Potter spell book, and reading stories about ancient gods and goddesses from cultures across the world. It's always so refreshing to view the world through the lens of a child.

Here some things you can do to bring a bit of comfy cozy magic to the children in your life. Note: *Always* ask permission of a child's parents before introducing witchcraft.

◊ Get outside. Nature is a great way to introduce children to a pagan or earth-based spiritual practice. Go for hikes, hunt for faeries, set up a nature scavenger hunt, create a notebook about the seasons, talk to animals.

◊ Craft the sabbats. Another wonderful way to involve children is by making crafts to celebrate the sabbat seasons. Carve pumpkins at Samhain, make a Yule log together to celebrate Yule, craft a Brigid's cross at Imbolc, decorate eggs for Ostara, make a mini maypole for Beltane, create flower crowns at Midsummer, bake bread together at Lammas, make a corn dolly at Mabon.

◊ Read together. Take a trip to your local library and pick up books on the great myths from cultures around the world—Greek, Egyptian, Roman, Celtic, etc. Spend time reading books that present witches in a positive light, unlike the wicked old crone depicted in pop culture.

◊ Involve children in rituals. My entire family performs rituals with me during most of the sabbats. At Yule we burn the log together, at Beltane we write our wishes for the summer season on long strings of ribbon and tie them to a tree in the backyard. At Mabon we create gratitude lists and share them with one another. At Samhain we light candles on the ancestor altar and share stories and memories about our passed loved ones.

Daily Mini Rituals

We've chatted a lot about bringing the magic into the everyday—through blessing our home, through cooking, through our gardens, through our sacred spaces—and now I want to add to those things and give you some small rituals you can do throughout your day to keep you connected to your practice, no matter how busy you are or how little time you may have.

If you can do just one of these magical check-in items a day, you're touching your practice in one way or another and bringing some magic to the mundane. You can do these things on their own or add them to a longer sacred daily ritual.

◊ Stir tea or coffee. After you've poured your morning cup of tea or coffee, enchant it with a simple stir (you don't even need to add sugar, cream, or spices). Say over your coffee, *"May this day be full of protection, abundance, and magic."* While speaking the words, draw a pentacle in the air with your finger or in the beverage with a spoon.

◊ Wear enchanted jewelry. Enchant a piece of jewelry (see below) that you wear often—your wedding ring, a favorite necklace or bracelet. Once you've enchanted a piece of jewelry, the simple act of placing it on yourself every day reminds you of your practice and of whatever intention you pour into it.

◊ Make a protection pouch. Create a protection pouch using comfrey and bay leaf dipped in rosemary essential oil. Place the dipped herbs in a small pouch and add a few chips of obsidian. Tie it to your rearview mirror, toss it in your purse or bag, or carry it on your person. (You can use different corresponding herbs and oils to create a pouch for any intention—safety, self-love, abundance, prosperity, and more. Directions given later in the chapter.)

◊ Meditate. How many times have I said meditate throughout this book? More than one hundred. Meditation is the basis of my practice and a foundation for elevating your magical crafting. Take any amount of time to check in with yourself through a quick meditation. This can be two minutes or twenty. Take a deep breath, close your eyes, and just be. (See chapter 6 for more meditation tips.) Just remember that meditation is a way to ground, and grounding is the basis for any magical working. Yes, I sound like a broken record with that one, but that's because I believe it so firmly.

◊ Intentionally light a candle. As soon as you wake up, light a white candle and invite your guides to join you for the day for your highest good. Take a few moments to envision how you'd like your day to unfold.

◊ Step outside. Connect with the earth by stepping outside (or open a window if you don't have easy access to the outdoors). Better yet— step in the grass, dirt, or sand in your bare feet and really ground yourself.

◊ Stretch. Raise your arms high over your head while inhaling deeply. Bring your arms down on the exhale. With each breath, imagine a vibrant white light surrounding you with goodness for the day.

◊ Speak with gratitude. While sipping on your morning beverage, take a few moments to say aloud what you're grateful for. It's even better if you write it down.

◊   Take a magical cleansing shower. While in the shower, envision the
    drops of water washing away any negative thoughts and energy that
    may be trapped in your aura.

◊   Play music. Create a playlist that puts you in a magical, joyful mood
    and play the songs while you're getting ready in the morning.

◊   Move. Exercise is a great way to raise energy and to honor your
    body. Take your workout routine outside for an extra boost of
    connectedness and natural magic.

◊   Pull a card. It takes only a moment to pull a tarot or oracle card for
    the day. Ask your guides to show you what you need to see for your
    highest good, draw a card, and meditate or journal for a moment or
    two on its possible meaning.

◊   Touch your altar. Even if you don't have a solid chunk of time
    to dedicate in front of your altar, touch it in one way or another.
    Simply touch the surface, run your finger over a candle, or say
    a quick blessing to a deity statue. These simple acts keep you
    connected to your practice, no matter how short they are.

◊   Get crafty. Take a moment to work on a crafty project, whether that
    be coloring a picture, doing some knot magic through knitting, or
    creating your very own wand.

◊   Read. Grab a copy of a book on a witchy topic that interests you.
    It you can't afford to drop dollars to purchase a book, head to the
    local library and check out a magical title. Try audiobooks if you're
    frequently on the go.

◊   Communicate. Check in with other like-minded friends, whether
    that be in person, on the phone, or through social media. I find that

when I'm in a bit of a spiritual funk, a few texts exchanged with a witchy friend is all I need to snap out of it.

◊ Make affirmations. Write down affirmations and speak them aloud or to yourself throughout the day. Write them on sticky notes and leave them around the house for you to find at a later time.

Item Enchantment Ritual for Protection

Enchant your favorite stone or some other trinket with protection and wear it or keep it someplace close to you.

You'll need:

black candle (white will work if you don't have access to a black candle)

item you wish to enchant

Light the candle and hold the item tightly in your hand. Imagine a white circle of light surrounding you and charge the item with protection by saying, *"I pour protection and love into this item. May protection surround and follow me wherever I go."* Repeat twice more. Continue visualizing the circle of protection around you for as long as you wish. Once finished, allow the candle to burn out.

Jewelry Enchantment Spell

Use this spell to enchant a favorite piece of jewelry with a particular intention or purpose.

You'll need:

a piece of your favorite jewelry

Choose an intention you'd like the piece of jewelry to have. Good health, protection, friendship, love, abundance, etc. Cleanse your space. Cast a circle or visualize a sacred space around you.

Hold the item in your left hand and place your right hand on top, covering the jewelry. Now pour your energy into it. Visualize the intention of your choosing, pouring it into that specific piece of jewelry. Connect an affirmation with this. *I am magic. I am safe. I feel loved and protected.*

Once you've charged the jewelry with an affirmation, say that affirmation each time you wear the piece. Any time you see or touch the jewelry, you'll be reminded of its power.

EVERYDAY SACHETS AND MAGICAL POUCHES

Sachets are small, enchanted pouches filled with herbs, oils, crystals, and other magical items that you can carry on you to remind you of a particular intention or to bring protection, abundance, love, luck, or other qualities to you.

Many witches hang sachets around their homes, properties, and gardens to attract magical qualities to those spaces. I love sachets because they're easy to create and pack a whole lot of magical punch in a small item.

All you need is cloth, twine (or cotton string), herbs, and oils. After you've created your sachet, hold it in your hands and charge it with its intended intention.

Abundance/money sachet: in a green cloth, combine aventurine chips, dried thyme and mint, and a drop of frankincense essential oil. Tie with twine and hang in your office or wherever it is you work or plan for work.

All-purpose sachet: in a white cloth, combine crystal quartz; dried basil, rosemary, and dill; and a drop of rosemary essential oil. Tie with twine and use anywhere you see fit.

Garden sachet: in a green cloth, combine citrine gemstone chips; dried basil, dill, sage, and calendula; and a drop of mint essential oil. Tie with twine and hang at the entrance of your garden.

Love sachet: in a red cloth, combine rose quartz chips, dried rose petals and rosehips, and a drop of rose essential oil. Tie with twine and hang it in your bathroom as a reminder of self-love and care or in the bedroom for a touch of love magic.

Protection sachet: in a black cloth, combine obsidian crystal chips; dried rosemary, mugwort, bay leaves, and mint; add a drop of cedar essential oil. Tie with twine and hang in the entrance of your home, in your car's glove compartment, or anywhere else you're in need of protection.

Sleep sachet: in lavender-colored cloth, combine amethyst crystal chips; dried lavender, rose, and chamomile; and five drops of lavender essential oil. Tie with twine and place under your pillow, on your nightstand, or hang over the head of your bed.

Blessed Be

Thank you for joining me for this comfy cozy chat on house witchcraft. It is
my hope that you've learned a bit and are excited about trying in your own
home some of the rituals, meditations, and recipes that have made mine
a place of comfy cozy magic for years. Through approaching the everyday
with an eye for the magical, we have the unique ability to nurture and
nourish the mind, body, and spirit of our homes, families, animals, visitors,
and more.

So no matter how busy you get, remember the small, meaningful things
you can do to bring magic into the everyday. Go clean that house, cook those
meals, celebrate those sabbats, partake in those rituals, dress those altars,
tend to those gardens, light those candles, cuddle under those blankets, and
sip on those cups of tea with your innate magic in mind.

After all, magic is all around us. If only we would look.

Blessed Be, my friends. Jennie

GLOSSARY

Throughout this book, you'll find words that may not be familiar to you, especially if you're newer to your practice. Refer to the words and definitions below to help you better understand some of the ritual and spell instructions in the book. Please keep in mind that these are my definitions for the following terms, and others' definitions may vary.

Affirmation: a positive, direct statement said aloud or silently to yourself; spoken in present tense and filled with intention

Altar: sacred space you go to for connection to spirit and to complete magical workings

Amulet: an object of protection that is charged to deflect specific negative energies or thoughtforms; they can be made of any sort of material, such as feathers, plants, beads, jewelry, a horseshoe, or a pentacle

At home: relaxed and comfortable; at ease; in harmony with the surroundings

Banishment: a form of defensive magic used to exorcise, or get rid of, a particular negative energy, spirit, or person

Bind: to magically restrain a person or entity from performing harmful or negative magic on you or on someone else

Chakras: the seven major energy centers within your body, including the crown, third eye, throat, heart, solar plexus, sacral, and root; chakras can be aligned through energy work and meditation

Charge: to load an object with a particular intention; often accomplished by holding the object in your hands and envisioning your magical will, energy, and intent pouring into it

Charm: a series of words (rhyming or not) used for a specific purpose, often in spellwork, as a blessing, or to enchant an item; also an item that has been charged with a specific intention or task

Cleansing: the removal of negative objects or energies from an item, place, or person by utilizing positive, high vibrational psychic energy

Consecrating: the act of blessing or charging an object, place, or person by instilling it with positive energy

Deosil: clockwise direction for casting a circle, stirring liquids, and inviting something in

Divination: the art of using magical tools and symbols to gather information from the universe, from deity, from your guides; examples of divination tools are runes, tarot and oracle cards, pendulums, and scrying

Evocation: to call something out from within yourself

Familiars: animal who has a spiritual bond with its witch and who takes part in magical workings; they are often sent to protect their owner

Grounding: a technique that brings you into the present moment meant to help you relax and prepare for magical workings

Home: the place where one lives permanently, especially as a member of a family or household

Invocation: the act of bringing something *in* from *without,* and calling something to you

Magic: the art and science of focusing your intention, emotions, will, and actions to make change in the world around you and within you; magic is neither good nor evil

Pentacle: a circle surrounding a five-pointed upright star that symbolizes a belief in witchcraft and the magic of the natural world; it's used in ceremony, protection, and ritual work, and the five points represent the five elements of earth, air, fire, water, and spirit

Ritual: a focused mental and/or physical ceremony to perform a specific magical work

Sabbats: the eight pagan celebrations honoring the seasonal turning of the wheel and corresponding festivals: Samhain, Yule, Imbolc, Ostara, Beltane, Litha, Lughnasadh/Lammas, and Mabon

Talisman: an object designed for a specific magical purpose

Ward: a defensive magical working used to protect and guard against negative energies of any kind by directing energy away from your space

Wheel of the Year: one full cycle of the seasonal year beginning with Samhain and going through Mabon (*see* Sabbats)

Wicca: a pagan religion that one is initiated into that worships both God and Goddess

Widdershins: working in a counterclockwise direction; you stir or turn widdershins to close a circle or when doing banishing work

Witch: any person who practices witchcraft and believes in a connection to nature and in using words, thoughts, and actions to create positive change

Working: the process of using magic to reach a desired positive goal; examples of working are spellwork, ritual, writing in a journal, meditating, and working with divination tools

Sources and Recommended Reading

Books

Adler, Margot. *Drawing Down the Moon: Witches, Druids, Goddess-Worshipers, and Other Pagans in America.* Penguin Group, 1979.

Albertsson, Alaric. *To Walk a Pagan Path: Practical Spirituality for Every Day.* Llewellyn Publications, 2013.

Auryn, Mat. *Psychic Witch: A Metaphysical Guide to Meditation, Magick, and Manifestation.* Llewellyn Publications, 2020.

Ballard, H. Byron. *Seasons of a Magical Life: A Pagan Path of Living.* Weiser Books, 2021.

Blake, Deborah. *Everyday Witchcraft: Making Time for Spirit in a Too-Busy World.* Llewellyn Publications, 2015.

———. *The Goddess Is in the Details: Wisdom for the Everyday Witch.* Llewellyn Publications, 2009.

Bradley, Kris. *Mrs. B's Guide to Household Witchery: Everyday Magic, Spells, and Recipes.* Weiser Books, 2012.

Brownell-Grogan, Barbara C. *Healing Herbs Handbook.* Sterling Publishing Company, 2018.

Campbell, Joseph, source TK

Cavendish, Lucy, and Serene Amber Conneeley. *The Book of Faery Magic.* Blessed Bee, 2010.

Cunningham, Scott. *Cunningham's Encyclopedia of Magical Herbs.* Llewellyn Publications, 1985.

———. *Earth Power: Techniques of Natural Magic.* Llewellyn Publications, 1983.

———. *The Truth about Witchcraft.* Llewellyn Publications, 1988.

Cunningham, Scott, and David Harrington. *The Magical Household: Spells and Rituals for the Home.* Llewellyn Publications, 2016.

Daimler, Morgan. *Fairycraft: Following the Path of Fairy Witchcraft.* John Hunt Publishing, 2016.

Dugan, Ellen. *Cottage Witchery: Natural Magick for Hearth and Home.* Llewellyn Publications, 2008.

Estés, Clarissa Pinkola. *Women Who Run with the Wolves: Myths and Stories of the Wild Woman Archetype.* Rider, 1992.

Franklin, Anna. *The Hearth Witch's Compendium: Magical and Natural Living for Every Day.* Llewellyn Publications, 2017.

Johnson, Cait. *Cooking Like a Goddess: Bringing Seasonal Magic into the Kitchen.* Healing Arts Press, 1997.

Kiernan, Anjou. *The Book of Altars and Sacred Spaces: How to Create Magical Spaces in Your Home for Ritual and Intention.* Fair Winds Press, 2020.

Knight, Sirona. *Celtic Traditions: Druids, Faeries, and Wiccan Rituals.* Citadel, 2001.

Kruse, John T. *Faery: A Guide to the Lore, Magic, and World of the Good Folk.* Llewellyn Publications, 2020.

Kynes, Sandra. *Llewellyn's Complete Book of Correspondences: A Comprehensive and Cross-Referenced Resource for Pagans and Wiccans.* Llewellyn Worldwide, 2013.

Llewellyn. *Llewellyn's Sabbat Almanac: Samhain 2010 to Mabon 2011.* Llewellyn Worldwide, 2010.

Mitchell, Mandy. *Hedgewitch Book of Days: Spells, Rituals, and Recipes for the Magical Year.* Red Wheel/Weiser, 2014.

Moura, Ann (Aoumiel). *Green Witchcraft: Folk Magic, Fairy Lore, and Herb Craft.* Llewellyn Publications, 2009.

Murphy-Hiscock, Arin. *The House Witch: Your Complete Guide to Creating a Magical Space with Rituals and Spells for Hearth and Home.* Adams Media, 2018.

Patterson, Rachel. *Curative Magic: A Witch's Guide to Self Discovery, Care, and Healing.* Llewellyn Publications, 2020.

RavenWolf, Silver. *To Ride a Silver Broomstick: New Generation Witchcraft.* Llewellyn Publications, 1997.

Starhawk. *The Earth Path: Grounding Your Spirit in the Rhythms of Nature.* HarperSanFrancisco, 2006.

———. *The Spiral Dance: A Rebirth of the Ancient Religion of the Great Goddess.* Harper & Row, 1979.

Stewart, Tenae. *The Modern Witch's Guide to Magickal Self-Care.* Skyhorse Publishing, 2020

Taylor, Astrea. *Intuitive Witchcraft: How to Use Intuition to Elevate Your Craft.* Llewellyn Publications, 2021.

West, Kate. *The Real Witches' Handbook: A Complete Introduction to the Craft for Both Young and Old.* Llewellyn Publications, 2008.

Whitehurst, Tess. *Magical Housekeeping: Simple Charms and Practical Tips for Creating a Harmonious Home.* Llewellyn Publications, 2010.

Websites

www.goddessandgreenman.co.uk
www.moodymoons.com
www.patheos.com

TO OUR READERS